George Patrick Fox

Fashion

The Power that Influences the World

George Patrick Fox

Fashion

The Power that Influences the World

ISBN/EAN: 9783337033736

Printed in Europe, USA, Canada, Australia, Japan

Cover: Foto ©Suzi / pixelio.de

More available books at **www.hansebooks.com**

FASHION:

THE POWER THAT INFLUENCES THE WORLD.

THE PHILOSOPHY

OF

Ancient and Modern Dress and Fashion,

BY

GEORGE P. FOX.

REVISED AND ENLARGED.

Series A. D. 1850, 1860, 1872.—Third Edition.

THE TRADE SUPPLIED BY

THE AMERICAN NEWS COMPANY, 115 TO 121 NASSAU STREET, N. Y.

SHELDON & CO.,
677 BROADWAY, UNDER GRAND CENTRAL HOTEL,
NEW YORK.

TRÜBNER & CO., 60 PATERNOSTER ROW,
LONDON.

Dedication.

To the

GOVERNMENT

AND THE

GALLANT PEOPLE

OF THE

UNITED STATES.

CONTENTS.

	PAGE
Dedication	ix
Preface	xvii
Introduction	xx

CHAPTER I.

The Philosophy of Modern Dress and Fashion . . 17

CHAPTER II.

Dress—17th to 19th Century 24

CHAPTER III.

Suggestions on the Diplomatic Dress of U. S. Ministers, Secretaries of Legation, and Consuls to Foreign Governments 37

CHAPTER IV.

Etiquette in Dress and Fashion 42

CHAPTER V.

The Dressing Gown and Lounging Jacket . . 44

CHAPTER VI.

The Morning Dress 45

CHAPTER VII.

The Riding Dress 48

CHAPTER VIII.

The Hunting Dress 50

CHAPTER IX.

Dinner Dress 51

CHAPTER X.

Evening Full Dress 53

CHAPTER XI.

Clerical Dress 56

CHAPTER XII.

Judicial Dress 58

CHAPTER XIII.

Collegiate Dress 60

CHAPTER XIV.

European and American Wedding Dress 61

CHAPTER XV.

Liveries 65

CHAPTER XVI.

Funeral Dress 67

CHAPTER XVII.

The Code of Fashionable Intercourse 69

CHAPTER XVIII.

The Drawing-Room Dress, etc. 80

CHAPTER XIX.

The Ball-Room Dress and Address 82

CHAPTER XX.

The Promenade Dress, etc. 85

CHAPTER XXI.

The Etiquette of Carriage and Equestrian Exercises, . . . 87

CHAPTER XXII.

The Etiquette of Courtship and Matrimony . . . 89

CHAPTER XXIII.

The Code of Commercial Intercourse 93

CHAPTER XXIV.

The Relation of the Buyer and the Seller 100

Supplementary Series.

Dress and Fashion from English Authors 107

Dress and Fashion—American Authors—Fashion . . 115

Dress and Fashion—American Authors—Costume . 120

A Star of Fashion—Bath, England, and Beau Nash, 130

Essays on Dress and Fashion, 1790–1868 . . . 135

Fashion and its Leaders 141

	PAGE
Of the Beauty of Colors	145
Form, Expression, Attitude	148
Dress and Fashion—Lord Chesterfield to his Son, etc.	159
The Emigrant—The Adopted Citizen of the United States, etc.	179
Correspondence and Notices of the Press, etc. . .	199–254

"We give it as our opinion that Mr. Fox's work on Dress and polite Address will command an immense circulation, both here and in Europe."—*New York Express.*

"The author handles the subject like an adept in polite and elegant literature."—*Washington City Correspondence.*

"Mr. Fox has given to the world an essay on modern Dress and Fashion of transcendental merit."—*London Saturday Review.*

"No polite gentleman, 'par excellence' can consistently do without the information upon Dress and Address contained in Mr. Geo. P. Fox's volume."—*Richmond Enquirer.*

"I heard there were two Presidents in the East Room,—the President of the United States and the President of Fashion, Mr. George P. Fox."

PREFACE.

> "Authors are judg'd by strange capricious rules,
> The great ones are thought mad, the small ones fools;
> Yet sure the best are most severely fated,
> For fools are only laugh'd at—wits are hated,
> Blockheads with reason men of sense abhor,
> But fool'gainst fool is barb'rous civil war,
> Why on all authors then should critics fall?
> Since some have wit, and shown no wit at all."—POPE.

IN promulgating a code for the government of fashionable intercourse there must necessarily be, more or less, an arbitrary style in its preparation, an authoritative diction to give it force and efficacy; and it is quite possible that this peculiarity may be noticed in the following pages. The author begs leave to state, that in the preparation of this work he has been actuated only by a desire to impart information where it is most needed, to inculcate the necessity of observing the requirements of fashionable society upon those who know the right and yet the wrong persue, in many points of dress and etiquette; and who are led into serious mistakes by those whom they are taught to regard as guides in their conduct in the polite circles of society.

Among other missions that this work is intended to perform may be mentioned chiefly the two following: The improvement of taste in general society and the offer of suggestions to those who are considered its leaders, on the duties which their position in the community requires. And 2d. To give such plain hints to those about to enter polite society that it will be impossible for them to go astray, if they rightly consider and improve upon the principles and philosophy of modern dress.

At the present day many men of wealth are inclined to pay more attention to the decoration of their houses than to the proper adornment of their persons. Thus, while they gladden the eye by beauty of architectural display and interior embellishment they nevertheless sadden the hearts of friends by a slovenly exhibition in the poor attire of their person. Reform is needed in this particular. And it is to be hoped that this work will be mainly instrumental in creating a more general desire for original taste, not only in the adornment of the house we dwell in, but in an equal consideration for the house in which we live, literally speaking, the body.

INTRODUCTION.

> "My dukedom to a beggarly denier,
> I do mistake my person all this while;
> Upon my life she finds, although I cannot,
> Myself to be a marvellous proper man.
> I'll have my chambers lined with looking-glasses,
> And entertain a score or two of tailors,
> To study fashions to adorn my body."—RICHARD III.

FASHION.

FASHION is and has been and will be, through all ages, the outward form through which the mind speaks to the material universe.

"It is a power which without concerted action, without either thought, law or religion, seems stronger than all of them."

We wear forms—we see forms—we like and dislike forms, places, shades and colors. Form and Fashion go hand in hand, links of the same harmonious chain creating all the outward life we live.

Fashion in all languages designs to make, shape, model, adapt, embellish and adorn. It has modelled society and shaped Empires; and has held in its scales the fates of kingdoms and the destinies of commonwealths. It has entered into the life of all nations and will be identified in its influence with our fortunes forever. So universal is its control that we cannot escape from its all-encircling embrace. Wherever we *go*, whatever we *do*, whatever we *are*, Fashion holds the wand of power over us, more blandly, but not less imperiously than the sceptre of empire was swayed by the Cæsars.

Fashion, then, means our outward life. Not merely the dress we wear, the latest dance for the festive hall, nor the style of carriage, or livery of the servant. It decides architecture, embellishing the Doric, the Ionic, the Corinthian, and the Cosmopolitan, taking a grander and higher form in the Roman.

In the Middle Ages it prescribed the Gothic, and the matchless structures of those periods which now amaze and delight the traveller, from the banks of the Rhine to the thousand glittering spires that shoot into heaven from that miracle of beauty, the Cathedral of Milan.

It dictates law for the just and the unjust; it influences the forms of worship, for it decorates the panels of the Christian Church, as well as those of the synagogue, the Turkish moslem, the Chinese pagoda, and dresses all priests and altars.

Fashion presides at every scene of life; from the cradle to the tomb its empire is unbroken. Its subjects are all mankind.

Dress is only one of the countless forms in which Fashion asserts her dominion. But in this great department especially, it is peculiarly the province of art to adapt and perfect form to nature and classic taste.

Inconsiderately as men sometimes speak of tailors, no painter or sculptor of any proficiency is ever heard to disparage the successful efforts of a good tailor. They know that the drapery on figures must fall gracefully, and harmonize with the shape and style of the subject; and it is one of the most difficult achievements of their arts to accomplish. It is just as true of the tailor and his profession.

In this respect the tailor with his shears, the author with his pen, the sculptor with his chisel, the painter with his pencil, or the genius that produces beautiful combinations abridging labor, while benefitting the laborer, stand on the same relative scale, each desirous of producing that which ennobles and adorns our common humanity.

Probably not one garment made in a hundred is a perfect fit. It is one of the most difficult arts in the world to dress a man perfectly. No matter what may be the prevailing fashion of dress, no two men are made near enough alike to be equally well-fitted by the same article; consequently a ready-made garment, cut for unknown or unseen figures, is, according to the law of good taste, an impossibility, and never did, nor ever will, grace the person of a gentleman of acquired taste. A difference in occupation, stature, form, attitude, complexion, or even manners, will decide the fabric and color of the garment best suited to each individual style; and a thousand combinations have patiently to be elaborated to produce that rare sight—a perfectly well-dressed gentleman.

If the author had not achieved this point of eminence in his art, he should regard his life as a grievous disappointment to his professional pride. He, however, depends not alone on his own assertions, but is indorsed by the highest and noblest in the land. His credentials are voluminous from the eminent living and departed. To quote the words of that great patriot and statesman, the illustrious Webster, "I heard that there were two presidents in the east room, the President of Fashion, Mr. George P. Fox, and the President of the United States, Mr. Millard Fillmore." *

> "Some with a flash begin and end in smoke;
> Others in smoke begin and bring forth glorious light,
> And without raising expectations high,
> Dazzle us with surprising miracles."

* The levee at the White House, Washington, D. C. (See notices of the press.)

PHILOSOPHY OF FASHION.

CHAPTER I.

THE PHILOSOPHY OF MODERN DRESS AND FASHION.

> "Only because I wore a threadbare suit,
> I was not worthy of a poor salute.
> A few good clothes put on with small ado,
> Purchase your knowledge and your kindred too."
> —HEYWOOD'S ROYAL KING.

A GREAT modern writer has no less profoundly than pointedly observed that "In the one universal subject of *clothes*, rightly understood, is included all that men have thought, done and dreamed. The whole external universe and all that it contains is but *clothing;* and the essence of all science lies in the philosophy of *clothes.*"

We regard dress not merely as an envelope of broadcloth, cassimere, silk, satin, or velvet, wrought up in more or less taste after the model of a prevailing pattern, but as one of the most significant expressions of character, and sustaining an intimate relation with manners and morals.

It is universally admitted that nothing marks the gentleman more than the style of his dress. The elegance, propriety and good taste which are conspicuous in that, at once create a presumption in his favor. They form a perpetual letter of recommendation whose validity is everywhere acknowledged. A rich and becoming costume answers as a passport to the traveller; opens the door of hospitable courtesy to the stranger; gives the citizen a free ticket to the best places in society; forms a decorous ornament to wealth, and where wealth is wanting, in many respects supplies its place. You notice the well dressed gentleman in the streets; in the most crowded thoroughfares he is conspicuous above the throng; he challenges your admiration even at a distance. "Far off his coming shines."

As he approaches, you are struck with the exquisite contour of his dress, the tasteful harmony of its colors, the charming smoothness and supple undulation of its fit; and you instinctively pronounce its wearer to be a gentleman. He has received justice at the hands of his tailor, and you cannot mistake the seal of his gentility.

Nor is the dress a less important indication of the personal taste of the wearer. It often marks the distinction between vulgarity and refinement; it shows the disposition no less clearly than language or conduct. A mind imbued with a love of elegance, devoted to the beautiful harmonies of form, of color, of motion; inspired with a passion for the becoming, the lovely, and the graceful, will not fail to manifest itself in selection and arrangements of dress. You see its innate love in its outward surroundings. Good taste is, in fact, like good music—it harmonizes and marks the whole man. It extends to the cut of a garment, no less than to the construction of an epic. We have always noticed that a polished mind was attached to graceful and elegant attire. We judge of the good taste of a man, not merely by his air and bearing, his speech and gesture, or his love of art and literature, but also and in a great measure by his dress. We have often been deceived by the one, seldom or never by the other. The character of the dress, moreover, is important as a sign of social position. The moralists say, a man is known by the company he keeps. We say he is better known by the clothes he wears. The air of good society cannot be given except by education, aided by the artistic hand of a genuine tailor.

The relation of dress to manners and morals is too obvious to be insisted on. The first condition of good manners is ease and self-confidence. If you have no self-respect, your manners cannot win the respect of your associates. If you are not easy with yourself, you can never make them easy with others. But can a man be at ease in a coat out at elbows, a coat which hangs like a meal-bag upon his shoulders, a coat which reminds you of a specimen of fossil remains, or an heirloom from one of the company in the ark, a coat which is a badge of contempt, a sign of vulgarity, an expression of a dilapidated purse, a careless disposition or an uncultivated and barbarous taste? No, an ill-dressed man must be ill at ease. His manners must be forced and ungraceful. He never can show that delightful suavity, that fascinating union of spirit and sweetness, that enchanting harmony of expression and movement which distinguish the finished gentleman unless he feels perfectly at home in his clothes, unless they have been fitted to his person, his character, and his physiognomy, with that exquisite skill which is essential to the style of manners, so finely described by the great orator Edmund Burke as the "unbought grace of life."

Our great American statesman, the late Daniel Webster, was no less distinguished for the graceful and imposing dignity of his manners than for his diplomatic skill and his commanding eloquence. But as he was the most able of constitutionalists, so was he one of the best dressed of gentlemen.

In the favorite costume, blue and buff, of an illustrious namesake of the author, the British commoner, Charles James Fox, no man appeared to more trandscendent advantage in a legislative hall or a fashionable drawing-room, than did the eminent expounder of the constitution; while on more solemn occasions these colors were doffed, to give place to the more sombre black mingled with white. We will not undertake to say in what degree he was indebted to the perfection of his dress for his imposing presence; but we do say that his dress gave an additional power to the majesty of his demeanor, and the weight of his eloquence.

We may quote his own words to this effect, when on donning a suit from the once celebrated emporium of Milton's (a retired tailor) he exclaimed, "Ah, I now breathe easier than I have done for a long time; indeed, I feel as if I were in Milton's Paradise regained."

The influence of dress on morals presents a theme for the pen of a philosopher; a merchant-tailor, however experienced, can scarcely hope to do it justice. We will, however, venture to submit, that no civilized man is apt to commit a crime in a good suit of clothes. An easy and graceful garment is incompatible with a deed of violence. The serenity produced by a perfect fitting suit puts one in good humor with all mankind. Arrayed in a fine and elegant costume, with the consummate polish of appearance which it is equally the duty and the pride of the conscientious artist tailor to impart, a man feels his responsibilities as a citizen, is inspired with a love of order, becomes refined and elevated in his tastes, is filled with respect for law, decorum and propriety, and finds in his own character a guarantee against temptation. Indeed, out of the immense number of customers who have honored the author with their patronage, we do not know of one who has ever been convicted of a crime.* Many we have seen raised by that influence to exalted stations. Not one has been brought before a court of justice; not one but who sustains a fair and estimable character, as an American citizen. Is it not evident that the secret of

* (Viz., up to 1860. *Multum in parvo.* More meant than meets the ear.)

virtue is often found in the wardrobe—that a good dress is a great preservative of good morals?

But we must not omit to mention the connection of dress with commerce, the importance of which cannot be overlooked in our mercantile community. The tailor and the dressmaker are indispensable media between the importing merchant and the consumer. They distribute the commodities which are furnished by commerce. Until the goods of the merchant have passed through their hands, their value is in a dormant state, and they contribute nothing to the embellishment or the utility of life. Patronize the tailor, you give an impulse to commerce; you help to keep open the great highway of nations; you lend your support to the most efficient and most indispensable agency of civilization. In seeking the taste and elegance of your own personal appearance, you not only contribute to the interests of the profession, but promote the welfare of our common country and universal fashion.

"Let Fashion follow the Treasures of the United States." *

Such, fellow-citizens, is the importance of a wise devotion to this branch of social economy. We maintain that you cannot overrate the value, and hence you perceive the necessity of availing yourselves of the aid of such artists as you can rely on for strength and fineness of fabric, elegance of fashion, color, perfection of fit and of finish.

* George P. Fox, at the Levee, Executive Mansion, Washington, D. C.

We are actuated, by a noble ambition, to elevate the uniform dress and costume of the age to its true place, in the unfathomed interest of the world of fashion; to make the American citizen as renowned for his garment as for his institutions; to cause Paris, London and Berlin to hide their diminished heads as arbiters of gentility; and to adorn the Doric simplicity of American principles by the inimitable grace and elegance of an appropriate cosmopolitan costume. While in no way anxious to curtail, but, on the contrary, wishing to increase the business of our fellow-citizens, our sole desire is to establish a style of fashion commensurate with the growing importance and dignity of this national Union.

CHAPTER II.

DRESS—17TH TO 19TH CENTURY.

"And catch the manners living as they rise,
Laugh where we must, be candid when we can."—POPE.

"And beauty advances with a single hair."

Queen Elizabeth—Dudley Earl of Essex — Sir Walter Raleigh—Lord Bacon—Chevalier Bayard—Cardinal Wolsey and Richelieu—General Washington.

ADORNMENT of the person appears, from ancient and modern testimony, to be an instinct of our nature. As a tribute of affection for those we love, we decorate our bodies to exhibit our appreciation of the heart. The earliest Greek sculpture known represents a lovely maiden twining a wreath of flowers in her lover's hair. The savage, in his native wilds, the South Sea-Islanders, and our own Aborigines, have their garments tastefully embroidered by those who love them, and in the civilized world the first gift of awakened affection is an ornament for the person of the loved one. Mothers, from the highest rank to the humblest walks of life, always have this sentiment, and exert their abilities and their means to dress their children to the greatest advantage, deeming rightly that, in so doing, they awakon sympathy in each maternal heart beating in unison with their own affections.

Despite the sarcasm levelled against dress by the unthinking and unappreciative, the subject has engaged the practical attention of some of the wisest and most celebrated men of all ages, nor has the study been unproductive of praiseworthy results. The sway maintained over the mind of Queen Elizabeth, by the celebrated Dudley, Earl of Essex, was by the exercise of his remarkable mental powers; and when he was reproved by his brother, the Earl of Suffolk, for the value he placed upon the adornment of his person, who said, "Parts like yours need no such vanities," replied: "The writings of a clerkly scribe takes not from the wisdom of the epistle, but rather tempts to a frequent perusal thereof. Why should a well-fashioned exterior, or a nice casket lessen the value of the jewel within it?" The Chevalier Bayard declared, under nearly similar circumstances, "that he who cared not for his personal appearance, cared not for his friends, or their opinions." The Cardinals Wolsey and Richelieu, Archbishop Fenelon, Sir Walter Raleigh, Lord Herbert, the celebrated George Villiers, Duke of Buckingham, the admirable Crichton, and many others of talent and distinction, are described by the authors of their times, as "marvelous proper men" in their dress, and its appropriateness and fashion. In one of the letters of the great Lord Bacon, in the Veralam collections, he writes: "The fashioner (tailor) hath made my gown of a color so unsuited to me as to make me appear sick, as if badly distempered." Thus proving that the great philosopher had in his mind an appreciation of the true aims of dress—its appropriateness of color to the complexion of the wearer. Dress, like every other thing in this life, is as commendable for its use as it is reprehensible for its abuse. Its uses and influences upon society are what all have attempted to prove, and it is hoped that the great names quoted above will rescue the subject from the shallow apology too often made its abuse,—that it is trifling and undeserving our study.

How material to our worldly interests a good exterior may become, is a matter of daily experience. Our first appearance before one upon whom our success in life in some degree depends, or before the opposite sex, in whom we seek a personal interest, often creates impressions favorable and beneficial beyond our fondest hopes, or may unjustly detract from our real merits, in a manner that requires much time and effort to obliterate, if they ever be completely removed. In this latter position, an ill-made suit of clothes, or unsuitable in color, may still more strongly turn the tide of opinion to our disadvantage, and in a manner we can scarcely conceive; and the common and unfriendly defence is, "Yes, Smith is a good fellow, when you know him, but he has no taste, and is quite a sloven in his dress." This must be regarded as anything but complimentary, in meeting the bad impressions already formed. Nor can such a state of things be looked upon as much less than a grievous fault, when the remedy is so easily in the reach of all. With the opposite sex, we keenly see and instantly detect the want of taste that detracts from their pleasing appearance. "What an indifferently dressed *girl* she is! Who would think that any one of Miss Jones' complexion could wear a blue or a green dress! It makes her look as yellow as saffron." These are the daily remarks of men, who are themselves guilty of the same solecisms of taste.

If a gentleman goes to an establishment, which has for its principal a man of taste, who knows his profession thoroughly, such defects would be instantly remedied.

An instance occurred a few years since, where a gentleman of fortune made an observation to the following effect, in an establishment on Broadway: "It is of no use, Mr. G. P. Fox, for me to care what I wear; nobody could make me look well. I must therefore depend upon other attractions, not upon dress, for the impression I am to make upon society." The reply was, "Will you permit me, sir, to select your dress, and leave its details altogether to my arrangement? If your friends and yourself are not satisfied with the result, which I am confident they will be, you will at least be no worse off." Laughingly, but doubtingly, the offer was accepted, and the specialties of complexion and bodily form were studied and overcome. A color suited to the complexion was chosen, the extreme length of neck was modified, the great fall of shoulders was remedied by the setting in of the sleeves and their surroundings, and in effecting these improvements an exact fit was for the first time applied to the form, giving a gentlemanly ease and freedom from all restraint, as pleasing as it was novel. His friends accosted him with, "Dear me, how remarkably well you look to-day. What have you been doing with yourself?" And his immediate relatives declared he was an altered man. With all the necessary attributes of mind and of fortune, he needed but this to place him upon an equality with those he had deemed more fortunate than himself in their external appearance.

The effect of the color of the clothing upon the complexion of the wearer can scarcely be credited by those who have not witnessed the fact and studied its causes. In some complexions one color and its various shades will produce a greenish tinge, and another color will bathe the same countenance with a violet tinge, whilst the contrast produced when the clothes are formed of a proper contrast of color will give to the face the ordinary healthy flesh tint. In suiting the clothing to the complexion of the wearer, a knowledge of colors and their modifications by contrast is absolutely essential. Where a shade of sallowness approaching to a yellow tinge pervades the countenance, if a light blue or green be worn, the natural tendency is to increase the sallowness almost to a yellow. If, on the contrary, shades of brown, particularly those having a tint of yellow mixed with red, be worn, the defect is so modified by the contrast as to be lost to the ordinary observer. Under such circumstances, in black full dress, the judicious introduction of the modifying tint near the face, will also serve to produce the desired contrast. Two cases in point may serve to illustrate the fact better than a more elaborate elucidation of the theory upon which the contrast is founded. The witty Colonel Kingsman, in the beginning of the present century, was in the height of his fame. Those who did not know him continually noticed the extraordinary yellowness of his face. One day a little girl, a spoiled child, asked him before the Prince of Wales, afterwards George the 4th, " Why have you a face like brass, Colonel?" The wit replied : " Because I am a man of metal, my love." But the attention brought upon him rankled in his mind, and caused him annoyance. Beau Brummell, who was one of the Colonel's most intimate friends, perceiving the effect produced, told him that if he would go with him to his tailor, who had taste and judgment, he would assist him in remedying the defect. Brummell's promise was fulfilled, and to such a degree, that the Prince's joke that Kingsman was the man with the brass mask completely lost its application. The well-known Lord Petersham (the late Earl of Harrington) was of a peculiarly sallow complexion, although otherwise a remarkably handsome man. To overcome this defect, his tailor invented that brown, now known as the " Harrington brown," in a full suit of which he was dressed for morning attire during his life. The effect of this brown, in overcoming the sallowness of his face, induced him to have his liveries of the same shade, and his carriages were painted of the same color. Brummell was a man of great talent as well as taste, and to him we are indebted for the frock-coat, which superseded the swallow-tailed dress-coat in morning costume; for the trowsers superseding the tight-fitting habiliments previously prevailing; for the broad-spread neckcloth; for making the black necktie fashionable, and for the introduction of starch into the white necktie. In his intimacy with the Prince of Wales he made those suggestions to the Prince that caused him to be the best dressed man—the first step toward being the first gentleman in Europe. Brummell was the first man to make fashions in some degree succumb to the requirements and peculiarities of the individual, and the color of dress to the complexion of the wearer. Count D'Orsay in recent days did not think it derogatory to his great and varied abilities to make dress his study, and indeed to become the leader of fashion in that particular, in England as well as on the continent of Europe; and with his large and generous heart, nothing gave him greater pleasure than suggesting the cut and color that would best become his friends, and put them upon good terms with themselves.

General Washington was celebrated for his noble appearance, majestic form, and intuitive taste in dress. The effect of the yellowish buff vest, small clothes linings and facings, and the gilt buttons of his blue uniform coat, in making it harmonize with the weather-beaten complexion of the hero, seems to have evinced an inborn taste and judgment rarely witnessed. When General Washington, as president, was dressed for his civic receptions, the richness of the material, black silk velvet and point lace ruffles, their admirable fit and the imposing presence, that adorned rather than was adorned by them, showed how sensibly alive he was to the harmony of his personal appearance. General Hamilton was also well known for his admirable taste in dress; and Washington's suite, or military family, as it was then the fashion to call them, took their initiative of taste in their costume from their great chief. Military uniform, however, has but a recent history in comparison with civic fashions. For many ages uniformity was impossible, the armies being composed of levies upon the Barons, who brought to their sovereigns quotas of men according to the extent of their domain. Besides this, the universal custom of wearing armor rendered it unnecessary. King Charles the First, of England, ordered the leather buff suits of the army to be made after one pattern. Charles 2d, some years after the restoration, ordered the scarlet coat to be the dress-coat of the army, and in his latter years of the royal guards. This uniform continued through the succeeding reigns of James, William of Orange and Anne, until the Duke of Marlborough, before the battle of Blenheim, did away with the cuirass which the great Napoleon restored to his heavy cavalry—the cuirassiers. The three-cornered hat, trimmed with lace, etc., the square coat with long waist, formed of scarlet cloth with gold lace, lined with buff, the corners turned up so as to display an angle of the lining, whilst small clothes and canvas leggins, reaching above the knees, were the dress of the army, which, with trifling modifications, lasted until after the breaking out of the American revolution. The great Washington chose a blue and buff uniform of a similar pattern for that of the continental troops. At first, this was confined to the staffs and some of the officers. Blue has now become the national uniform, and the handsome contrast of blue shaded colors, so pleasing to the eye and becoming to the martial wearer, has engrafted itself upon the hearts of the people, and is inseparably associated with the father of his country and its heroic defenders.*

Up to the last few years the convenience of the soldiers, or the fitness of the form of the regimental to the duties of his avocation, entered very little into the thoughts of those who contrived new uniforms. George the 4th, when Prince Regent for more than twenty years, undertook the task of composing uniforms, caps, helmets, shockos, casquettes, jackets, coatees and pelisses, changed from day to day, truss-

* For a more detailed description of the "regulations and dress of the U. S. Army and Navy," the reader is respectfully referred to the books issued by the War and Navy Departments, containing elaborate drawings, official descriptions and orders by the Department of State at Washington, D. C. The practical experience of the author respectfully suggests that the fabrics for the U. S. service should be free from shoddy, in material and otherwise; and that all woven woolen materials shall be water repellant, warranted not to shrink or fade in color. U. S. N. for distinction, known as the darkest blue. U. S. A. of a lighter shade, viz.: no third shade. It is further suggested that, U. S. Volunteer Regiments, Zouaves and soldiers, be clothed in like manner. Choose fancy fast colors, each and all soldiers, and others in the service, suitably dressed in the same exact shade of material. The arms and accoutrements, &c., all to exact certified latest approved pattern.

ing up the soldier like a pigeon stuffed for roasting, and dressing him so tightly, that each manœuvre created a fear in the beholder that their garments would be split in pieces. In 1817 the Duke of Wellington introduced trousers into the army, but could not, before the end of a long life, get the tunic or frock-coat to supplant the tight-fitting bodycoat. The French first saw that the wide trousers and roomy tunic gave the soldier an immense advantage, and freedom from restraint while on duty. England followed, and we are gradually following a similar plan.

There might be introduced many improvements in military uniforms, and its readier adaptation to the freedom and graceful appearance of the wearer, the details of which can not be gone into in a brief essay like this, but which would come home immediately to the mind of the educated soldier, whose conservative prejudices have not fossilized his judgment. Although the gold lace and embroidery of Europe are not copied by us to a great extent, yet both arms of the service have been the victims of expensive and injudicious changes, in which caprice, in many instances, rather than judgment, has guided their invention.

In the navies of England and France, great changes have taken place for the last two centuries. In the first named country, blue, faced with white, has been used until lately, and in the latter, red, with gold lace, &c. King William the 4th altered the facings of the British Navy to red, for a brief period, but ultimately restored it.

The uniform and dress of the United States Navy were originally very simple: a blue dress suit, with epaulettes, the navy button, and a chapeau, being all that distinguished it from that of the civilian. This gave way some years since to more apparent distinctions of rank, by the distribution of the buttons, and a number of gold bands, &c., around the cuffs. In the month of March, 1852, the Navy Department issued a regulation order, for a change in the uniform and dress of the service. Each grade of commissioned officers, including the Marine Corps, were obliged to have undress, service, and full dress uniforms—the last richly ornamented with gold lace or embroidery on the collar, epaulettes, lace on the cuffs and pantaloons, according to rank, having on them the insignia of the particular grade in the service, with swords, chapeau, &c., to match. This costly uniform completely eclipses the modest dress of the army.

Various alterations have been effected by the successive secretaries of the army and navy. The principal one, however, in the navy uniform, has been in the abolishing of the body or full dress uniform coat. Whenever this latter change has been discussed, among distinguished naval commanders, it has always been with the popular opinion against that change. A partial restoration of the uniform dress coat has been made in favor of certain specified ranks in the service, especially referred to in the printed regulations of the Navy Department, for the year 1869, &c. Uniform and dress of the Revenue Marine Service has also been issued by the

Secretary of the Treasury. The allusions here made to the uniforms of the respective services of the United States are necessarily brief. The author, for a more elaborate description, would refer the reader to the regulations issued by the departments of the respective services.

The latter remarks are equally applicable in reference to the uniform and dress of the State of New York Militia, and other State Volunteer Militia, their uniforms being distinctive, soldier-like and efficient, yet different to the regular army of the United States. The uniforms of the New York Metropolitan Police Force, and Fire Department, are also obliged to conform to the printed regulations of the services here related.

For reasons stated, it is not the author's intention to describe in this edition minutely every article that is considered requisite or fashionable for a gentleman's dress, of the present day; it would require, to do the latter subject justice, at least many other volumes, containing pictorial illustrations, commonly called plates of fashion, with explanatory printed descriptions of gentlemen's under and outward attire, in manner similar to those that are regularly published in this country, France, England, Germany, &c. The fashion plates are generally accompanied with what is called tailors' paper patterns, and directions showing, to a certain extent, and giving a rough idea of the various modifications each garment is supposed to require, to harmonize in taste, cut, style, trimmings, fabrics, shades, and colors, deemed suitable, all of which are more or less useful for the guidance of the tailor and his customers, in the formation of civilian dress costume, the Army, the Navy, Liveries, &c.

Many of the leading fashionable tailors here import with their fabrics, viz., cloths, cassimeres, vestings, &c., plates of fashions, also suits of clothes, overcoats, &c.; the latter from some of the most celebrated tailors of France, Germany, England, and other parts of Europe.

The inventive genius and enterprise of the Americans being proverbial, they at once discard the incongruities, antiquated, stiff, formal, vulgar character of the European made clothes, and originate in their stead new styles of improved patterns, combining the advantages of the foreign made garments, in the superior adaptation of construction, gracefulness, ease and faultless finish, the admitted character of the American Standard of Fashion.

CHAPTER III.

SUGGESTIONS ON THE DIPLOMATIC DRESS OF U. S. MINISTERS, SECRETARIES OF LEGATION, AND CONSULS TO FOREIGN GOVERNMENTS.

> If I had served my God with but half the zeal
> I have served my king,
> He would not thus have deserted me
> In mine old age.—SHAKESPEARE.

THERE exists a great diversity of opinion among civilians, as well as officials, of what should constitute the costumes of our diplomatic representatives abroad. Many support the views of the late Mr. Marcy, when holding the office of Secretary of State. These views were, that an American representative at a foreign court, should appear in the simple dress of an American citizen, viz.: a black cloth suit. The contrast of this garb with the brilliant surroundings of uniforms and court costumes, makes the wearer appear as if he had suddenly come from a funeral ceremony into a gay assemblage. Besides, it presents the representative of the great American Republic, in the relation to the rest of the guests, of being mistaken for one of the subordinate waiters. (See index of contents and correspondence.)

It has been remarked by those who are far more competent to judge than the late Hon. Mr. Marcy, that such a dress is as much out of place in a court as he was. Some of our most enlightened citizens who have been presented at the various courts of Europe consider the above objections. They are equally supported by our Foreign Ministers, Secretaries of Legations and Consuls. Both parties most cordially agree, that the objections could be easily obviated without incurring the prejudices of the people, but on the other hand, eliciting their patriotic approval. It has been appropriately suggested, that the costume of the father of his country, as he appeared on state occasions, would be a suitable one for our Foreign Ministers. This consisted of a full suit of black silk velvet, with knee breeches, silk hose and dress pumps, frilled shirt ruffled cuffs, and court dress sword. The same high authorities also recommend that a similar suit, with modifications, be worn by the Secretary of Legation—yet of so marked a character as to distinguish him from his chief; and that the costume of U. S. Consuls should be governed by the regulation of dress as described in the archives of the State Department. The author has been favored by the State Department with a description of the official costume of the consuls, from which he quotes as follows: A single-breasted coat of blue cloth, with a standing collar and ten navy buttons in front. Vest of white Marseilles or buff cassimere; pants of blue cloth or cassimere, with gold lace down the outer seams. With this dress a cocked hat and small sword are to be worn.

The diplomatic and consulate service had, from the commencement of the Republic, a rich but unobtrusive dress, worn by them at foreign courts. This had the high sanction of General Washington, who is said to have half-chided Dr. Franklin for not wearing it, saying, "That he should uphold the dignity of his country, even in the eyes of fools." Governor Marcy, finding means of distinction difficult, hit upon the idea of improving and superseding the orders of the Father of his Country, by forbidding its continuance.

While the ancient close-fitting vestments exhibited all the bodily defects to which the physical form was subject, the fashioner of judgment of the present day can make the clothes of each individual meet the specialties of the occa-occasion. A few instances of ordinary variation from the true and perfect form will come to the daily experience of the reader. The shoulder on the right side has its muscles alone developed by many of the occupations of citizens, making the left shoulder appear lower and smaller. This is successfully obviated by the skilful artist, as is partially shown in the case of our late illustrious Commander in-Chief, General Scott, whose left shoulder receded from the effects of a wound received in battle, the ball from a British musket remaining under his blade-bone. By the manner in which the writer met and overcame this difficulty, it would be all but impossible to detect upon which side the variation was perceptible, and in thus remedying the defect, ease, grace and equality of form to the frame was restored.

A hollowness under the arms by the side of the chest, is very common with those not leading an active life. This can be as easily and skilfully remedied. The flatness and protuberance of the chest can be similarly obviated so as to give perfect grace to the figure.

By judicious cutting, and a knowledge of formation, the tall, slight man can be preserved from invidious comparisons, and the short and stout individual can equally be relieved from his peculiarity of appearance. If the limbs are inclined to meet at the knees, by the peculiar cut of the pantaloons, this defect can be concealed as when the limbs incline to bow; by another modification of this system, this defect can also be relieved from observation. So also what is termed buck-knees, similar to Richard the 3d, can be as easily concealed. A case in point was presented some years since in the alterations effected in the appearance of a well-known British Minister at Washington. This distinguished gentleman's limbs were peculiarly attenuated and formless, and when the author was called upon by him, the ambassador wore a dress which was most painful to look upon. But the first pair of trousers made for his lordship by the oriental system of cutting, instantly removed these peculiarities, and placed him on a par with the best dressed and best formed members of the Foreign Legation, &c.

In Paris, the fame of the Duke de Noailles and the Marquis de Valmy, as Chief de la Mode, arose from the exact adaptation of form, cut and color, to their personal requirements and peculiarities. The present Prince of Wales—although from his fair complexion and symmetrical form being released from the rules pertaining to exceptional cases—is remarkable for his taste and chaste neatness of costume. Fashion, they say, is an exacting tyrant, but like many other despots of modern days, it has been obliged to modify its requirements to the wants of the world, as the sole means of saving itself from a disgraceful dethronement.

To be neatly and appropriately dressed is undoubtedly our duty as it is our interest. If we would seek the world's respect, provided we have the means, let the materials be the best of their kind—this will be found the truest and wisest economy in the end.

Let your clothes fit nicely to the form, be appropriate in color, and well placed, as the bird arranges his feathers. In the business man this insures additional trust and confidence. He who cares for his own rights is seldom insensible to those of others. To our friends we are as much morally bound to offer a pleasing exterior, as a smiling face or a clean, well-appointed table. In the family circle it teaches our children order, cleanliness, and a love for the proprieties of life, and last, but not least, it gives a man a confidence in himself, and ease of manners in society, without which it is difficult for him to pass as a gentleman, or he of the slovenly dress to be recognized as one.

CHAPTER IV.

ETIQUETTE IN DRESS AND FASHION.

"Dress makes the man, the want of it the fellow,
And all the rest is leather and prunella."
"Costly thy habit as thy purse can buy,
But not expressed in fancy, rich, not gaudy,
For the apparel oft proclaims the man."

ETIQUETTE in dress and fashion is founded upon the all-important data, viz. : What is due to ourselves in the position we hold in society, and what we owe to those who have a claim on our respect, and in whom we are in daily intercourse.

From the time of the patriarchs to the present day, all nations of the world have had their ceremonial vestments, and despite the sneers of the cynic and the diatribes of the disorganizers of the social system, the best bred people of the civilized world have distinguished themselves from the under classes by the preservation of customs so easy of practice, and which convey to the intelligent mind the assurance, that he who faithfully observes the minor morals of society is rarely deficient in its more important virtues.

The Italian says, "Show me your company, and I will tell

you who you are." "Respect yourself as the first step to the respect of others." This axiom aptly applies to our daily dress, upon which we will now note down a few standard rules, gathered from the best society and authors in this and other countries.

CHAPTER V.

THE DRESSING GOWN AND LOUNGING JACKET.

"And your gown's a most rare fashion."—MUCH ADO ABOUT NOTHING.
"A fellow that hath had losses, and one that hath two gowns,
And everything handsome about him."—*Ibid.*

This luxurious *robe de chambre* was intended for the dressing room or chamber only, but heads of families have occasionally used it as a breakfast habit in their houses. The gentleman of true refinement before visitors, would not appear so costumed. The wearing of this robe infers that the toilet is not thoroughly made, a fact which implies no great respect for the visitor so received. A lady might, with as much propriety, appear in curl papers at breakfast, as a gentleman in a dressing gown. Young men often appear at the breakfast table in a tasty, easy fitting and fancy trimmed lounging or smoking room jacket. It is not correct to wear this garment (*a robe de chambre*) at any other meal, and certainly not in the drawing-rooms or parlors, in presence of polite society.

CHAPTER VI.

THE MORNING DRESS.

"Methinks I scent the morning air."
"The morning cock crew loud."
HAMLET.

In the cities, the general morning or walking dress is that in which the man of refinement appears at the breakfast table, the restriction in colors being in regard to black, except the party is in deep mourning, or belongs to the learned profession, where the sombre shade is always allowable, or in case the complexion of the wearer imperiously prevents his adoption of light or fancy colors. In the first circles of Europe, it is in a high degree bad taste for a gentleman to appear in the street during the morning in black pantaloons. It is always best that the morning dress be in a manner *negligé*, and the rule which prohibits the introduction of every portion of full dress in the early part of the day, is also imperative in rendering inadmissible the appearance of the morning frock coat upon promenade, at or after dinner, or in dress circles. Sack and frock coats of various colors and forms, to suit the person and complexion of the wearer, with vest and pantaloons to match in shade, or of the same or similar material, forming an agreeable contrast; scrupulously white linen, black or colored neck-tie of modest pattern and becoming shade, white pocket-handkerchief with colored border, form the morning costume of the gentlemen under fifty years of age, after which period more quiet colors and contrasts become suitable. The office or promenade suit of one color throughout, with appliances as above stated, is also strictly within the rule. In a morning costume, kid gloves of any fashionable material, from a stone-color to a dark olive-color, according to taste, are worn.

> Have a good hat; the secret of your looks
> Lies with the beaver in Canadian brooks.
> Virtue may flourish in an old cravat,
> But man and nature scorn the shocking hat.
>
> O. W. HOLMES.

The hat which may be worn now varies so much in shape and color, that all that can be said upon that subject is, that the wearer should select according to the season, fashion, and most suitable to his countenance. In the city of New York, as the Central Park has become the afternoon promenade of the *beau monde*, taking the place on this continent of the Champs Elysée, Hyde Park and Kensington Gardens of Europe. Gentlemen who accompany ladies of refined taste and education, should not appear in office suits, but should assume a dress more conformable to the respect which they owe to the opposite sex. A blue, brown, fancy dark color, mixed or black frock coat, a silk or velvet vest, fancy cassimere pantaloons, would be appropriate. With this dress, varied according to the season, primrose, lavender and light fawn-colored gloves, are according to rule.

CHAPTER VII.

THE RIDING DRESS.

A horse, a horse, my kingdom for a horse!
                               RICHARD III.

THE riding dress for equestrian exercise differs in cut, color and material from that used for walking. The coat is usually cut away at the skirts, with cross pockets in the skirt and breast. The pantaloons or trowsers are occasionally differently formed, and so arranged as to be put within the high boots used on horseback. Overcoats and Oriental Khabans are of various kinds of fabrics and colors, according to the season; the dress or closely-fitting habit being almost superseded, except for dress occasions, by the loose *negligé* garments of the period.

The travelling dress, which may be classed with morning attire, should be of some of the various shades of brown, gray, or mingled fashionable colors, which do not show the dust, and when used, leave partial or no trace of travel about them. A light texture duster over-garment is commonly worn in travelling in summer.

In the country, during the summer, the various thin fabrics of wool, which are made to be worn that season, are preferable, according to climate, to linen, being more healthful, as well as more pleasing to the eye. In the fall or winter, the shooting dress should consist of a brown, grey or mixed-colored cloth, of a firm but elastic texture, with convenient and suitable pockets. The trowsers loose and full; but it is an advantage to have them so made as to be during stormy weather, conveniently put within the Zouave gaiters or long boots.

CHAPTER VIII.

THE HUNTING DRESS.

> Better to hunt in fields for health unbought,
> Than fee the doctor for a nauseous draught.
> ANON.

PERHAPS there is no costume in a gentleman's wardrobe that is more to be admired than that worn by the English hunter. Arrayed in a brilliant scarlet riding coat, buskin breeches, top boots, cap, spurs and whip, he presents a picture of manliness, courage and joyous hilarity, which is delightful to behold. The incidents of the hunt are beautiful and exciting in the highest degree—the full pack of hounds in full pursuit, making the woods resound with the music and choruses of the chase. The sport is one that strengthens the man and invigorates the horse, and is recognized as one of the most manly that gentlemen of true taste can enjoy.

CHAPTER IX.

DINNER DRESS AND ADDRESS.

"The various cares in one great point combine,
The business of their lives is—*to dine.*"
YOUNG.

IN the family circle, and at our great and fashionable hotels, the full dress, which, a quarter of a century ago, was deemed indispensable where ladies appeared at table, has gradually given place to the *demi-mode,* dark frock coat, silk vest, dark pantaloons, black necktie, and plain white handkerchief. At all formal dinners, where invitations have been issued for some days previous to the event, the dress will differ but little from that of the ball room, one of the essential points of difference being, that the dress coat is indispensable while the white necktie is not. At many of our first-class hotels, individuals who claim to be considered fashionable appear among ladies at a late dinner in motley colored coarse office suits, giving rise to the pardonable suspicion that they have no other clothes besides; paying a very equivocal compliment to the fair sex, and setting a bad example to the rising generation, who are unfortunately too prone in their immaturity of judgment to show disrespect, imagining it a proof of independence. Officers in the Army and Navy are always expected to appear at dinner where there are ladies, in full dress uniform. Undress in the evening would be quite inexcusable in them.

CHAPTER X.

> "Come to our fete, and bring with thee
> Thy newest, best embroidery.
> Come to our fete, and show again
> That sky-blue coat, thou pink of men,
> Which charmed all eyes, who last surveyed it,
> And Brummel's self inquired, 'Who made it?'"

Evening Full Dress

Has always consisted of the most elegant and appropriate costume the taste of the epoch could devise. In ancient times, restrictions of color and materials were unknown, and so continue in the civil costume, in the court circles of the European sovereigns. Black and blue coats have, however, superseded all others in the best society. Forty years ago, small clothes and silk stockings, or light-colored pantaloons, were invariably worn; since that time the black trousers or pantaloons has superseded all other dress in that particular.

The celebrated "golden ball" introduced black velvet suits, with steel buttons and wrist ruffles. This fashion lasted from 1819 to 1822, when it yielded to various shades of a rich purple or brown, with steel buttons, which in their turn, in a few years, subsided into the present fashion. The evening dress, universally adopted by the fashionable world, is as follows: A black or blue fine cloth dress-coat, lined with black silk, plain or watered pattern, the blue coat having gold or gilt buttons; with the black coat, a cut or figured velvet, plain or figured silk or satin, or white silk, satin or cassimere vest; with the blue coat, buff cassimere, white Marseilles, plain or figured silk vest is appropriate; black cassimere pantaloons, dress boots or shoes, with lace hose, white oriental tinted neckcloth, and white shade kid gloves, are indispensable in the ball-room. In opera costumes, a black neck-tie, lemon or light buff gloves, may be worn, more particularly where the gentleman does not accompany ladies. In evening costume, the cambric handkerchief should be purely white. The shirt front should be of the finest material, but those to whom is conceded the first place, for good taste and fashion, eschew all other ornaments to it other than the fine stitch or embroidery. Studs, brilliants or pearls, are not unfashionable. As to the use of jewelry, it is difficult to decide how far its adoption is within good taste, but all ostentatious display should be studiously avoided.

The man of fine breeding is anxious to avoid any display that could be deemed vulgar, from which charge the mere costliness of the jewel could not relieve him, whilst a gem of art displays a taste and refinement of judgment that the vulgar can never rival. In all our endeavors to please, by our appearance and dress, the adaptation of our costume to peculiarities of form becomes the first consideration, and to all men of sense, the praise conveyed in the small sentence, " He is a well-dressed man," is a compliment to his judgment, instinct of taste and propriety, that the philosopher need not despise.

It is to be hoped that the beautiful blue coat, and gold or gold gilt buttons, with the buff vest, for evening costume, will be restored as the dress of Americans—colors so emblematic of those under which the independence of our country was won.

CHAPTER XI.

CLERICAL DRESS.

> Avoid thee, fiend, with cruel hand,
> Shake not the dying sinner's sand;
> Oh! look, my son, upon yon sign,
> Of thy Redeemer's grace divine,
> Oh! think on faith and bliss.—SCOTT.

A SPECIAL dress for the clergy has been, until within the last forty years, universal. In France, Italy, Spain, Canada, and America, including other countries, the Catholic clergy wear the ancient clerical costume of the sutan and cassock, with black bands, occasionally edged with white, as their ordinary dress. In the United States, with the exceptions, the custom does not prevail, and they are only distinguished from the civilians by a black frock coat, with a standing collar. The ministers of the Episcopal Church used to dress in a straight cut coat, vest buttoning up to the throat, made of thick corded black silk, white neck-cloth, small clothes and black silk stockings, or long black gaiters. The hat was looped up at the sides, leaving the brim wider in front than at the back; and if the wearer belonged to the dignity of a D.D., a silk ribbon noose was placed on the hat-band in front. Added to this dress, bishops and deans wore silk aprons. The ministers of the various denominations have been particular in their dress, except the Quakers and the Methodists, who have been remarkable for their plainness. The vestments of the Catholic clergy never vary, and need no immediate description here. Of the Episcopal Church, the black silk gown, the cassock, the surplice and the hoods and scarfs can scarcely be said to have any uniformity, varying in some particulars in different diocese.

The clergy should be known by their habitual dress, which should be of black, and uniform in its character. A black single breasted frock coat, reaching to the knees, with standing collar, black cassimere pantaloons or trowsers, plain black or corded silk vest, cut in the old ecclesiastical style, would form a becoming and appropriate costume. The Bishops might be distinguished by a nearer approach to the court-shaped coat. The Catholic clergy might resume the ancient sutan, as in most other nations of the world. This dress is both dignified and graceful; it fits the form to the waist; hence it is full and reaches to the ancle, and is buttoned from the throat to the end of the skirt, by a row of closely set buttons.

CHAPTER XII.

"Freedom of the press, freedom of person under the protection of habeas corpus, and trial by juries impartially selected."—JEFFERSON.

JUDICIAL DRESS.

"In the hands of men truly great, the pen is mightier than the sword." We say that the shears are more powerful than either, or both, because the shears conquer woman, and woman is the mother of all mankind.

Washington was anxious to retain the old judicial dress, that has come to us from the mother country. Some of his coadjutors opposed this, upon the ground that the robe did not constitute the man a better or more faithful judge. Washington replied: "Nor does the uniform make a soldier, but it is a distinction of which the soldier is honestly proud;" and he prevailed in keeping the black silk gown and black court suit, as the official costume of the judges of the United States Supreme Court. We see, without dissent, the clergy of various denominations wearing the clerical gown and bands. We almost enforce black as the clerical garb, and yet we tolerate any colored dress in our supreme and superior courts of law. Formerly the New York sheriff wore a sword and cockade. Later, all the sheriffs, and deputy sheriffs, upon the occasion of the execution of criminals, wear a solid gold badge and locust baton. The United States marshals, and others, a badge as the emblem of his authority. Then why should not our legal functionaries wear that distinctive garb, which all other civilized nations have adopted, and preserved to this day? If the judges of the higher tribunals dressed in black suits, with silk robes of the same color, it would certainly add to their appearance and dignity, and be a badge to their high office, which is now needed.

CHAPTER XIII.

"Stores of learning bring we home,
Brought from school and college."
"Make we them a heaven on earth."—HEBER.

COLLEGIATE DRESS

WAS universal in the colleges before the revolution. Columbia College, in New York, and Harvard, in Cambridge, Mass., are some of the places which have preserved the custom, and this only in a limited degree. At the commencements, the under-graduates of Columbia College wear the black silk collegiate gown, and the Oxford cap. At Harvard, the gown alone is worn, but its use is optional with the students. In Canada, until lately, the full collegiate costume was worn at the three universities, the same as in those of Europe.

CHAPTER XIV.

EUROPEAN AND AMERICAN WEDDING DRESS.

> Oh, come ye in peace, or come ye in war,
> Or to dance at our bridal, young Lord Lochinvar?
> The bride kissed the goblet, the knight took it up,
> He quaffed off the wine and threw down the cup.
> He took her soft hand ere her mother could bar;
> "Now tread we a measure," quoth young Lochinvar. —SCOTT.

As it is to be hoped that the great event of matrimony will form but one epoch in a man's life, so ought it to be correspondingly joyful and celebrated. The gayest costume has been adopted by both sexes in all nations for the celebration of a wedding, while those who acted the principal role have used as much white as could be introduced into the wedding habits. At the present day, the man of taste and fashion wears the following wedding dress: a blue dress coat, sometimes lined with white watered silk, with fancy gold or gold gilt buttons, a white figured satin or silk vest, cream colored fine cassimere pantaloons, fine white silk or lace hose, and full dress thin shoes in summer and dress boots in the winter, white kid gloves, and white plain handkerchief. All the first-class nobility of Europe are thus dressed on this important occasion, at a wedding. In all but the Northern States of our Union, a dislike, almost amounting to a horror, of black for the dress of the bridegroom seems to pervade *élite* society, and if the appropriately emblematic be good taste, nothing could be more fitting for the event than the dress quoted above—blue, the color of hope, and white, the emblem of purity and truth. The groomsmen should be dressed as nearly as possible in the same style. Black, at least, should not be worn. If in the summer, blue dress coat with gold or gilt buttons, white Marseilles vest, white satin or jean pantaloons with shoes or light dress boots, would be appropriate and complimentary to the occasion. The same dress with black cassimere pantaloons in the fall or winter would be in good taste.

> " Music arose with its voluptuous swell,
> Soft eyes looked love to eyes which spake again,
> And all went merry as a marriage bell."—BYRON.

AMERICAN WEDDING DRESS.—The bridegroom usually wears a very fine black cloth (blue nevertheless recommended), dress body coat lined with white silk or black satin, according to the taste of the wearer; white figured silk or satin dress vest, fine black dress cassimere pantaloons, (occasionally pearl drab pantaloons are worn,) white kid gloves, plain white lawn, figured silk or satin necktie, patent leather boots, all made in the height of fashion. It is usual for from one to six groomsmen to be in attendance, all dressed precisely the same as the bridegroom, distinguished by wearing a white rosette bordered with gold or ribbon on the breast of the coat. Where the lady has a father and mother, the father accompanies her to church, the bridegroom escorting the mother of the bride. The bridesmaids and groomsmen follow immediately in the rear, first, second, third and fourth (in couples) or as the case may be. In the absence of the father, some near male relative gives the bride away. On entering the church the bridegroom joins the bride, she leaning on his left arm, the bridesmaids and groomsmen next. The father and mother of the bride, or the friend who gives away the bride follow immediately after they advance to where the clergyman is standing, the first bridesmaid taking her position in line to the left of the bride. The first groomsman proceeds to the right of the bridegroom, and so on until all are in line with the bride and bridegroom. Either at church or in the parlor, the ceremony is the same. When the ring is used, it is the duty of the first bridesmaid to remove the glove from the left hand of the bride, and hold the same until the ceremony of placing the ring is completed by the minister. After the benediction is pronounced, the bridegroom immediately salutes the bride. The entire party retire in the same manner in which they came. If there is a reception at the house, congratulations are not to be offered in the church, excepting by the clergyman. The friends reserve their compliments until the bridal party arrive at home. It is then the immediate duty of groomsmen in attendance to meet the guests as they arrive, introducing each by name to the bride and bridegroom.

The friends so calling upon the bride should bring with them their own visiting cards and hand the same when met by the groomsmen. The cards are afterwards placed upon the receiver, so that the bride and bridegroom can see whom to call upon in return. When the wedding takes place at the house it is the duty of the groomsman to send a carriage for the officiating clergyman, accompanied by one of the groomsmen or a near friend duly authorized to act in his stead. This is the proper time to hand the clergymen his fee, sealed in an envelope or placed in a suitable purse. The amount of the fee is invariably left to the generosity of the bridegroom, according to the circumstances. It is not unusual for an additional offering to be given to the clergyman by the father of the bride.

CHAPTER XV.

LIVERIES.

"Verily, I swear 'tis better to be lowly born,
And range with humble livers in content,
Than to be perked up in glistering grief,
And wear a golden sorrow."—KING HENRY VIII.

"Apparel them all in one livery."
—KING HENRY VI., Part II.

THE custom of dressing retainers and domestics in the livery of the family they serve is of great antiquity. The Venetian patricians did so as early as the year 980. The adoption of coats of arms was the occasion of the custom, which was brought into England by the Normans in 1080. The coat that covered the armor was emblazoned with the armorial bearings of the wearer, and as the vizor of his helmet covered his face, and armor was usually made of one pattern, this was the only means by which his followers could distinguish their leader from the other knights fighting with him. The livery consisted of the principal color and metal of the arms, and usually floated in the streamers in the back of the helmet of the chief. Thus in the arms of the family of Hamilton, the ground is red with three white cinque upon it. The streamers were consequently white and red, and such is the livery of that ancient family to this day. The arms of the Campbells of Argyle are a gyrony of eight pieces, gold and black; the streamers are of the same, and the livery chocolate (which liveries take the place of black) turned up with yellow. The footman of the Hamiltons wears a court shaped white coat, collar and lining of scarlet, with silver buttons having the crest or arms upon them, red vest, and small clothes, white stockings and shoes with silver buckles. The coat of the coachman is of the frock shape, that of the grooms the same, only shorter; the coachman's dress in all but the coat is the same as the footman's; the grooms wear top boots and leather small clothes. In the United States, a simple livery has prevailed, more resembling the morning or undress livery of the noble families of Europe, such as a drab, gray, green medley or blue coat with the livery buttons; a vest with the color of the arms.

CHAPTER XVI.

FUNERAL DRESS.

"The solitary, silent, solemn scene,
Where Cæsars, heroes, peasants lie
Blended in dust together; where the insulting proud
Resigns his power, the miser drops his hoard,
Where human folly sleeps."—DYER.

UPON this occasion, full mourning must be worn by the near relatives of the deceased. This consists of a black dress coat, cassimere vest, and pantaloons of the same color. At the funeral formerly, the costume was a black silk band, with large ends, around the hat, and a scarf of the same material, across the right shoulder, the ends on the left side tied with ribbon; the more distant relatives and friends of the deceased had the scarf of lute-string silk. If the deceased was young and unmarried, the hat bands and scarfs were of white lawn, or linen; the weed or crape on the hat worn by a widower reached within an inch and a half of the top of the hat; for a parent, the depth of the hat band being somewhat less, the other relatives remaining in mourning for three months; the handkerchief is bordered with purple or black; the gloves in undress are black, purple or slate color, and in full dress, pearl gray or lavender, sewed with black.

Mourning should be worn, as we are told by a professed authority,

"For a husband or wife, from one to two years, though some widows retain mourning for life.

"For a parent or grandparent, from six months to a year.

"For children above ten years of age, from six months to a year; for those below that age, from three to six months; for an infant, six or seven weeks.

"For brothers and sisters, six to eight months.

"For cousins, or uncles, or aunts, related by marriage, from six weeks to three months.

"For more distant relatives or friends, from three weeks to as many months, according to the degree of intimacy."

"The servants are ordinarily put in mourning, by those who can afford it, on the death of an important member of the family. The nurse only in the case of the death of young children."

CHAPTER XVII.

THE CODE OF FASHIONABLE INTERCOURSE.

"Let's do it after the Roman fashion."—ANTHONY AND CLEOPATRA.
"Oh! visionary as the airy dagger of Macbeth, yet absolute as the law of the Medes, is this omniscient goddess of our nether world—this insuperable ruler of our destinies—Fashion."

WHEN a great French wit and philosopher was asked what constituted a true gentleman, he replied: "He who has the most easy and graceful manner of unostentatiously demonstrating a good heart." In this sentence is summed up all that society calls upon her children to observe towards each other, and all its rules of government are but manifestations of this one great principle. He who derives not pleasure from the happiness of those about him, is no true gentleman, nor is it possible for a gentleman to be regardless of the feelings of those with whom he associates. It thus appears that the "primum mobile" of the well-bred man of fashion is the hope of his own rights being respected in return for the respect shown to the rights of others. It is easier to go happy through the world than is generally credited; and selfishness, egotism and self-conceited indulgence in youth, have proven the source of more mischief to individuals, and pain to society, than the unthinking can conceive. In fact, good breeding and faultless gentleman-like demeanor are the offspring of a kindly heart.

Shaftesbury once wrote that "the taste for beauty and the relish for what is decent, just and amiable, perfects the character of the gentleman and the philosopher; and the study of such a taste or relish will ever be the great employment and concern of him who covets as well to be wise and good as agreeable and polite."

"In no country in the world are general good manners so indispensable as in this democratic country. In Europe, where, in society, as at the railway stations, different classes are recognized and kept apart by insurmountable barriers and vigilant guards, it is possible, if you happen to be among the high-bred "firsts," or decent "seconds," to endure the existence of the unruly "thirds." These last, in fact, when viewed at a convenient remoteness of distance, are not without their interest.

"Their unkempt hair, blotched and greasy suits, rude manners, and coarse vernacular, are parts of the European picture, and by their homely manners, as well as the contrast they afford to the brilliancy of their superiors, seem essential to its effects. To look at a rough and unwashed, from safe distance, of European social distinction, by which he is toned down to the picturesqueness of one of Murillo's lousy beggar boys, is one thing; it is quite another, however, to have him at your elbow on railway and at hotel where you can hear, feel, and smell him. It is obvious, therefore, that the rough and dirty are quite out of place in this country, where, if they exist, they are sure to be close at your side. Universal cleanliness and good manners are essential to a pure democracy. This must be generally recognized and acted upon, or the refined will seek in other countries the exclusiveness which will secure for them that nicety of life essential to its enjoyment, and we shall be left alone, to wallow in our own brutality and foulness.

"There is no reason why propriety of manners should not be as general in the United States, as it is exclusive in most countries. With our facility of mixture, any leaven we have can be easily made to pervade the whole mass. There is no vested right, in this country at least, in decency and cleanliness. We can all be, if we please, what we are so fond of calling ourselves, gentlemen and ladies."—*Book of Decorum*.

The gentleman, *par excellence*, enters society with the desire to please and be pleased; in fact to pay in kind the gratification he seeks. A code of implied rather than written laws, have by universal consent of the fashionable world of all nations, been formed to carry out its intentions. An especial aptitude for application of these laws seems, to the casual observer, to be of greater facility in some nations than others—hence we say he is as polite as a Frenchman, and when we hear an individual condemn politeness and good breeding in others, it may be taken as a self-accusation on his part of some habitual violation of good manners or equal justice. The laws of good breeding may be aptly called, "The philosophy of social intercourse." In this country, the better observances of society are too often encroached upon by an under-current of political or commercial influences, which are not apparent on their face, but which are immediately perceived when pointed out by the close observer.

"The Americans have followed to some, though not to this absurd extent, the example of their trans-Atlantic relatives. We are by no means so reserved as they. Democratic friction has necessarily broken up and rubbed off a good deal of the original crustiness of our nature. Casual intercourse between strangers in America is much more free than in England. The American is as wanting, as the Englishman is abounding in reserve. The proper medium is between familiarity and resistance. In travelling, English constraint is often fatal to the general ease and cheerfulness, while American freedom is not seldom subversive of personal comfort. In the close proximity of a railway carriage, two persons can make themselves mutually agreeable, without any sacrifice of personal dignity, and it is certainly their duty to do so. The concessions on all such occasions are, of course, to be considered temporary. They are drafts at sight on each other's courtesy, to be paid at date, and received as a final settlement, which bars all ulterior clauses. The Americans generally are too indiscriminate in their introductions. They seldom allow two strangers to be together a moment without introducing them to each other. No presentations should be made without a regard to the mutual fitness and probable acceptability of the acquaintanceship about to be formed."

One of these influences may be seen in the indiscriminate introductions so commonly made, and which are intended by the introducer to be taken as future claims upon the acquaintance of his special friends.

> "Friendship is a plant the growth of every clime;
> Happy is the man that can rear a few."

This renders an introduction, leading to intercourse between friends, a matter of some difficulty, and causes great stress to be laid on the sincerity of its intentions. The admitted laws of the best society governing the introduction of one gentleman to another, are simple: The mutual friend asks the older or more influential of those to be brought together, if he has any objection to be introduced to Mr. ——. and if both assent, then the introduction takes place. It may happen that without this mode of proceeding, great embarrassment may be produced. Upon entering a drawing-room, all personal resentments against those you may find there must cease. Every true gentleman owes it to society not to bring his quarrels to disturb the peace of those who have never offended him. The accomplished gentleman never makes personal or invidious remarks upon any one in the company in which he may find himself. All who hear such remarks are displeased, and naturally imagine that their turn to be censured or ridiculed may come next.

Every person meeting at the house of a mutual friend, is upon an equality with those present, and has a right to address any member of the company without an introduction. When they have quitted the house, there exists no right of acquaintance, without a formal introduction by mutual consent.

Upon entering a drawing-room, the invited guest seeks the lady of the house, and bows to her. At assemblies, balls, and large parties, it is not incumbent on him to take leave of her upon his departure, but after a dinner party a bow is made to the host and hostess on taking leave of them. The day after the party, it is etiquette to pay the compliment of leaving your card at the house of your entertainer.

Never offer your hand to a lady. It is her place to offer hers to you, if the intimacy will warrant it, and if she should not do so, you must not think yourself slighted. It is probably an option on her part, upon which she is sole judge. At a dinner party, the guest conducts to the table such lady as the host introduces him to. He hands her to a chair, and takes a seat beside and to the left of her. Some tact is required by an entertainer to bring those together who will be congenial to each other, for upon such a circumstance depends the happiness of those present, and the success of the entertainment. Where there are several strangers at table, the commencement of the conversation is necessarily much restrained. Some pleasant anecdote or witty remark, free from all personal reflections, produces a smile, and banishes reserve, and enables the host, with a little tact, to put conversation into a channel that will make the entertainment a true feast. Never become a lecturer at the dinner table; never talk of yourself, nor let your anecdotes be personal; lead the conversation into subjects that, if all cannot converse upon, they may at least all feel an interest in. Politics, religion, or any subject that might produce acrimony of feeling, all personal references to private individuals, their dress, manners, eccentricities, or deficiencies, are repugnant to good breeding, and betray an ignorance of the best society, as well as a paucity of judgment and kindness of heart in the author. You have no right to constitute yourself the *censor morum* and corrector of the violations of strict decorum in society. The polished gentleman will show his distaste for unpalatable comments or satirical remarks, by making no reply to them, and turning the conversation to some more appropriate theme. This he should do without look or gesture, implying a rebuke to the person with whom he was conversing. The gentleman who is known always to act as above stated, soon relieves himself from being the recipient of scandal, and this even without losing the respect of him whom he so delicately rebukes. He or she who tells you a scandalous tale, pays you the equivocal compliment of believing that your own conscience needs to be flattered by a comparison with the faults of your friends to quiet its own accusations. Conversational powers are not given alike to all, and it must be remembered that good and appreciative listeners are admirable adjuncts to those who have the art of entertaining a party. A little tact and observation will give a facility in bringing out the mines of wit and joyous humor in many, who, without a fostering care, would remain hidden from society. As the true gentleman purchases his rank by his acknowledgment of and deference to the rights of others, so should he, however witty and well-informed, not usurp more than his fair share of the conversation. If some at table are particularly dull, or their attempts at wit fail of achieving success, his resumption of the conversation is a paid compliment of a higher appreciation of the preceding example. If a guest is particularly amusing, do not praise him by any compliment to his talent or powers, nor thank him for the entertainment he has afforded; it is both ill-bred and unnecessary to do so. The pleasure and reward awarded to such a person has been amply repaid by the gratification which he has been able to contribute to those around him. The man of refinement shrinks from being looked upon as a professional jester.

Let your attention at table be equally shown to all near you, particularly to the ladies. Learn to carve well, and know the delicate parts of game and fowl, that you may be able to distribute them amongst as many of your guests as possible; this is necessary, for, although all may not be able to appreciate them, yet none are insensible to the compliment which the attention displays as a mark of personal consideration. However good a jest, or witty a story may be, if it ever, in the remotest degree, brings ridicule upon religion, it should be by all means avoided. Such jokes are most unbecoming for a gentleman; they wound the feelings of the good, and are fraught with danger to the young and thoughtless. Your deportment at table cannot be wrong when you keep in mind the duties which you owe to those around you. It would be condescension to assume that the children of respectable parents should be informed why they should not use their own knives to cut the food which others are to eat; to eat with the knife instead of the fork, to take the delicacies at the table to the exclusion of others, and similar *gaucheries;* for to such, the end of becoming ornaments to society is all but impossible. In your attentions to others, ostentation is always vulgar; let your acts be spontaneous, and the rights and happiness of those around you the inspiring cause. Offer the best to those at your table, but never press them to take anything which they have once declined; your own taste is not that of your guest in every particular. If you offer wine to one who declares that "he tastes no intoxicating drinks," do not presume to term his abstinence a folly, for in nine cases out of ten it is fortunate for his friends and himself that he has made such a resolution. Be most cautious never to quote yourself as an example of superior morals. People will always think of Fénélon's maxim, "That no man is so tenacious of his possessions as he who has a doubt as to his right to them." The custom of inviting persons to drink wine with you has partially gone out of fashion. Indeed it was necessary to protect the host, but if you be asked by one who does not know the fact, do not refuse. You need do no more than put the glass to your lips. There is nothing more vulgar in society, than doubting the facts related in a jest, or anecdote, or any attempt at correcting the narrator in any part of the story, or declaring it to be old and well known. You have not with you the sympathy of the party, and it is a well-known fact that these marplots seldom add anything to the pleasures of social intercourse. Do not make a laughing-stock of any one in the company, however ridiculous he may appear. The only rebuke allowable to a bore, is to let his dulness pass without attention, and the most inveterate dullard looses courage when he finds himself without listeners. Never press any one to relate a story or witticism, or sing, and if asked yourself, you should speedily conclude if it would be acceptable, or otherwise, and decide accordingly. Ask no one to sing or speak whom you know to be incompetent. No gentleman inflicts pain upon society by giving annoyance to one of its members. Never solicit the opinions of those present upon the singing, or playing abilities of one who has been solicited to entertain the company, and always remember, that if he was not perfect in his efforts, he had shown a disposition in endeavoring to please. Be cautious only to laugh and applaud in the right place. Do not interrupt another while speaking; if your friend be prosy, let him serve as an example to be avoided.

CHAPTER XVIII.

In the drawing-room the conversation will be broken into coteries, and you will have the opportunity of selecting that most congenial to your taste. If a lady is led to the pianoforte to sing or play, listen to her, at least, in silence, and remember that if the execution fall below your standard, the longest *cantata* or *concerto* never lasted over five minutes, and cheerfully sacrifice that brief period. Never join in pressing the timid or reluctant to sing. If you succeed, you will seldom be repaid for your trouble; for confidence is so necessary to success, that without it, talent sinks into mediocrity; besides, it is unkind to inflict pain on a nervous temperament. If you have not a good knowledge of the fine arts, do not assume a critical and favorable judgment of the works of your host or hostess. It may elicit a severe criticism from those better informed, to the pain of those whom you thought to please. If you wish to praise, simply say it pleases you; this leaves your taste and not the work to be questioned. If the conversation in the drawing-room be upon literary subjects, never dogmatize nor make your praise or blame suggestive, and let your observations be as brief as circumstances will allow. If you are not prepared to speak from experience upon the topic under discussion, elicit information by suggestion to those better informed. By this plan, judiciously carried out, great and profitable pleasure may be elicited. Never stigmatize as useless the studies and pursuits of any man, but remember that they who are best informed, obtain their knowledge from the many toiling intellects which have been engaged for a life upon special studies. The well-informed gentleman will never raise a discussion in society that could excite heated arguments. His suggestions should alone lead to eliciting the truth upon scientific and literary matters. Upon all subjects in which the faculties of observation are called forth, the fair sex have a great advantage over the other, as they have also in affairs of the heart. A moderately well-informed lady is, therefore, far in advance of gentlemen upon these subjects, and much may be learned from her. In the reflective faculties man is generally in advance of woman. If gentlemen of mind would mildly discourage the propensity of young ladies to make dress and the peculiarities of their acquaintances their drawing-room conversation, they would prefer silence to losing the respect of the other sex; few men of sense choose a foolish wife, and as few would refuse a discreetly silent and amiable one.

CHAPTER XIX.

THE BALL-ROOM DRESS AND ADDRESS.

"On with the dance, let joy be unconfined,
No sleep till morn, when youth and pleasure meet,
To chase the glowing hours, with flying feet."—BYRON.

Many of the foregoing remarks are as applicable to the ball-room as the drawing-room. There, also, conversation is in parties, and, at intervals, between the gentleman and his partner. If a lady exhibits great vanity, the impulse to compliment her is almost irresistible, but it should be avoided; you should endeavor to lead the conversation into other channels, incidental to the occasion,—the drama, the opera, music, etc. When a gentleman seeks to be introduced to a lady for the purpose of dancing with her, she may, without offence to him, refuse the mediation of his friend in the matter. If a gentleman, who is casually acquainted with a lady, ask her to dance and she declines, he would understand that some affair of the heart stands in the way, and he affably assents to her wishes. If a lady should forget an engagement she had made and should accept another gentleman, and if he should not relinquish her hand upon an intimation of the fact, as he is bound to do, the man of true gentlemanly feeling yields with grace, and seeks the cause of the mistake in order to divest her of her embarrassment. In fact every gentleman is bound to avoid scenes in public, and they who sacrifice the comfort of a lady to their resentments in an assembly, should be avoided by both sexes. Never address a young lady as "Miss" without her Christian or surname added; it is a footman's politeness. Madam is applicable to both single and married ladies, but if you do not know the name, inform yourself before you address her. A gentleman should not ask a lady to dance with him several times in the same evening; it is embarrassing to her and her friends. To ask a lady twice is as much as a considerate gentleman should do. If a gentleman is paying attention to a lady, and is not engaged to her, he would not be justified in engrossing her whole attention in the ball-room; it holds her up to painful observation, and renders her liable to invidious remarks, if no engagement follows, and places him in the odious light of a male flirt. After dancing with a lady, conduct her to a seat near her family or *chaperone*, and leave her with a bow when her hand is claimed for the succeeding dance. Never dance with a lady without light kid gloves; never swing your partner round in the dance, nor be guilty of any other breach of etiquette that will subject her to impertinent remarks, or make her conspicuous. If much pleased with a lady, you may ask her mother's permission to call upon her the following day. If she reply, "We are seldom at home," or any other observation that does not imply consent, there the acquaintance must cease, a polite refusal being implied. In handing a lady to her carriage, bow to her immediately as she enters; to detain her in conversation, or any time exposed to the air, after leaving a heated ball-room, might endanger her health.

"Welcome the coming and hasten the departing guest."
"Genteel in personage,
Conduct and equipage."—CAREY.

CHAPTER XX.

THE PROMENADE DRESS.

"Awkward, embarrassed, stiff, without the skill
 Of moving gracefully, or standing still;
 One leg as if suspicious of his brother,
 Desirous seems to run away from t'other."—CHURCHILL.

WHEN ladies are walking alone, unless they be near relatives or intimate friends, the recognition must come first from them to the gentleman. If they do not recognize him he has no cause for offence; it is a right which he cannot call in question. If ladies are with a father or brother, then they are visible to all who know them, and may be addressed. When accompanying ladies in a promenade, it is not the custom to offer to them your arm in the United States, although the reverse is the fashion throughout Europe; and a lady walking by your side without your arm, would give great offence to her friends, and be deemed an unpardonable omission. In assisting a lady into her carriage, you offer her your right arm, and necessarily disengage her skirts from any little impediment.

In walking with a lady through the streets, place her on the inside of the walk to protect her from annoyance; gentlemen walking with ladies should not observe any little insolence that may occur that would subject her to annoying observation. They may be grateful for your energy and courage, but will avoid trusting themselves with you a second time.

CHAPTER XXI.

THE ETIQUETTE OF CARRIAGE AND EQUESTRIAN EXERCISES.

"But Coach! Coach! Coach!
Oh, for a coach, ye gods!"—CAREY.

" He does allot for every exercise
A sev'ral hour, for sloth, the nurse of vices
And rust of action, is a stranger to him."—MASSINGER.

THE gentleman having handed the lady into the carriage in the manner before mentioned, places her farthest from the open door, and seats himself beside her; if there are two ladies, he sits opposite to them, giving them the rear seats. In accompanying a lady on horseback, some little skill is necessary in assisting her in seating herself gracefully and conveniently in her saddle. The lady having disengaged her feet from the riding-habit, takes the reins in her right hand, holding her robes in the left. She puts her hand upon the shoulder of the horse, and, slightly raising the left foot, the gentleman gently assists her to vault into the saddle. As soon as she has arranged her position upon the saddle, the gentleman places the stirrup upon the left foot, and then arranges her drapery, in windy weather, fastening it under her feet, with a shawl pin. Some taste and tact are required in doing this last service, so as to leave the skirt free and graceful. In dismounting, you take the broach from the skirt and release the left foot from being encumbered by the habit. The lady disengages herself from the pomel of the saddle, and, standing in the stirrup, the gentleman takes her by the waist with both hands, and whilst she makes her skirts shorter, assists her to reach the ground. Whilst riding with a lady, place her horse on your right; it is easier for her to converse with you on that side than on the other. Always accommodate the pace of your horse to that of the lady's; if, however, you are riding by a line of carriages, you must place your fair charge farthest from the vehicles.

CHAPTER XXII.

THE ETIQUETTE OF COURTSHIP AND MATRIMONY.

"Oh, the days are gone when beauty bright my heart's chain wove,
When the dream of life, from morn to night, was love, still love.
Oh, flowers may bloom, and skies may gleam with purer, brighter beam,
But there's nothing half so sweet in life as love's young dream."

By all the laws of Society, a gentleman of true principles has a right to ascertain the physical and moral and mental qualifications of a young lady, before he commits himself to a courtship, from which an honorable man finds a difficulty in disengaging himself. The course a true gentleman should pursue under such circumstances, is to observe the respect and attention due to the lady and her family. We are bound not to permit an innocent and unsuspecting girl to remain one day without parental advice and protection in this most trying epoch in her life. So soon as a gentleman feels that the sentiment a young lady has inspired in him may lead to an ultimate union, he should make known his wishes to her father, and ask if his attentions meet with the approval of her parents. This is necessary upon two grounds; it is due to them, and will prevent the pain of a refusal and consequent disappointment, which might occur at a more advanced period. In the United States the customs attending courtships differ materially from those of Europe. For the actual happiness of both parties, the gentleman should not take the lady out riding in a carriage alone or on horseback, until an actual engagement has taken place. So long as fashion sanctions a young man in his attentions to the lady of his choice, he should observe that punctilious demeanor towards her, as not to compromise her in society. Parents love their daughters dearly, that they fear as much to have their affections blighted, as they do to have their fame called in question. The educated and conscientious gentleman of mature judgment, the high-toned man of honor, would never tempt an unsuspecting girl to elope with him; in so doing, he risks his reputation, and their own happiness, while he gives the severest blow to that of her parents, who he must remember are entitled to her first confidence and his respect. The daughter may be forgiven after a lapse of time, but the act can never be justified.

The polite gentleman should be well assured that he possesses the lady's love before he asks her hand. If the lady refuse him, he should allow no resentment, however much his feelings may suffer. Where so important and solemn a step as a fate for life is decided on, the lady should have the right of full reflection, and if a doubt of ultimate happiness should cross her mind, she has a full justification, at the last hour, in declining the proffered hand. If the lady be a flirt, the gentleman may well rejoice, instead of grieving that he has avoided an unhappy union.

If a gentleman of refinement really loves a lady, and deems her worthy of his love, he will never use words of endearment, or nauseous love-terms, towards her in society. After an engagement, each calling the other by the Christian name, is sufficient proof of mutual confidence and attachment; besides, true and delicate love is as jealous of the expression of its affection as it is of its reciprocal truth.

The purpose of this brief recapitulation of the code of fashionable intercourse is to show its moral and humanitarian influences upon society, and that all good breeding is derived from the truest of all philosophical data. Our own happiness is secured by the promotion of the happiness of those with whom we are associated; the toleration of the impulses and passions of our nature, and the deficiency of reason which at times should control them, have served to unsettle much of the grace and harmony of society. In a community of equal social and political rights, where the wily politician seeks, through the passions or prejudices of men, to ride into power upon the influence they create, a large amount of mischief must be occasioned by their unnatural excitement. Refined society should prove that the exercise of wisdom, in restraining our passions within the correct limits, constitutes the truest happiness, and to teach us that to ensure felicity, we must respect the rights of all, and share them in common.

The duty of the man of fashion, and of honor, is to curb these excitements, and to promote the influence of reason in society, so as to overcome all obstacles to its complete harmony, thus proving incontestibly that a good heart and a love of honesty, equal justice and equal rights, are the only true foundations of real politeness and gentleman-like demeanor, and thereby influencing a nation's happiness by the laws of fashion.

Separate the knave from the honest man, the counterfeit from the genuine, by understood signs, private badges, numbers and recognized recorded signals, credentials, distinguishing, in a word, the best from the worst species of mankind.

CHAPTER XXIII.

THE CODE OF COMMERCIAL INTERCOURSE.

" Factors in the trading world are what ambassadors are in the political world; they negotiate affairs, conclude treaties, and maintain a good correspondence between those wealthy societies of men that are divided from one another by seas and oceans, or live on the different extremes of a continent."—ADDISON.

THE duty that man owes to society, whilst performing either the part of the seller or the buyer of any legitimate article of trade, is the subject we now propose to discuss. We use the words buyer and seller in their most comprehensive terms, including what are denominated the learned professions, as well as those which are generally considered inferior employments. In a word, comprehending all dealings between man and man, where value gives call for value received.

The whole civilized world will admit as the test and standard of that duty the great Christian maxim: "Do unto others as you would they should do unto you;" that is, deal fairly, honestly, truthfully, and independently, without dissimulation, prevarication, or subterfuge of any kind whatsoever. Do no man a wrong or ungentlemanly act.

In the very constitution of society there is an absolute necessity for the relations of buyer and seller, and we therefore find records of the fact throughout the pages of both sacred and profane history from the earliest date.

In those records we trace, on the one hand, the noble character of those who, in the emphatic language of the Scriptures, deal justly; and, on the other, of those who delight in false weights and measures, and who, in the same impressive language, are said to be an abomination to the Lord. Honesty, then, may be considered as the main point in commercial intercourse.

In reviewing the career of nations or individuals, we may trace almost all the ills which have befallen them to some dereliction from the plain and straight road of honesty, truthfulness and fair dealing. Corrupt policy, and an inordinate greed of gain among politicians, is almost invariably the cause of a nation's downfall, and the same remark holds good in the case of individuals. "He that gathereth by labor shall increase," we are told on the highest authority, not he who endeavors to obtain fortune by defrauding his neighbor. Labor, whether mental or physical, represents and possesses a certain standard value, and, if properly applied, must at all times meet its reward. To achieve success on the road of life, we must set forth with the full understanding that it is no easy task which lies before us. There are mountains of toil and trouble over which we have to climb, and deserts of uncertainty across which our weary feet must pass. But with honor and honesty set before us, as our golden rule and guiding star, we shall not fail to reach the haven of our heart's desire. Nor are there any branches of trade or professions which may be considered as too trivial or insignificant for this rule of guidance. The star of honor shines with equal brilliancy, whether displayed in the drawing-room, the camp, or in the counting-house, and if not receiving from our fellow-men the same loud and enthusiastic greeting, will not fail eventually to receive its just recognition.

Pope beautifully expresses the character of the upright dealer in that celebrated line:

"An honest man's the noblest work of God."

And Burns, in one of his songs that has attained a world-wide celebrity, speaks of him as occupying a higher rank in the scale of Nature's nobility than could be conferred by the greatest of earthly potentates.

"A king can make a belted knight,
A marquis, duke, and a' that,
But an honest man's above his might,
Gude faith he maunna fa' that;
For a' that and a' that,
Their dignities and a' that,
The pith of sense, the pride of worth,
Are higher ranks for a' that."

A distinguished philanthrophist, in a pamphlet issued on the Religion of Reason, commenting on the words: "Therefore, all things whatsoever ye would that men should do unto you, do you even so unto them," says: "It is honesty he enjoins in these words. It is true that to be honest, as the world goes, is to be one man found in one thousand." Yet, when met with, strict integrity always commands respect even in rogues. A man correctly understanding himself, is a fool to be dishonest. Though nearly all persons, with scarcely an exception, will agree to endorse the principles as above set forth, when particular cases are brought to their notice, there will be as many different opinions as exist in the mental and moral characteristics of the men. It is therefore necessary that we should define more strictly, in an introductory form, what all conceive to be the precise rule and standard of honesty

This rule and this standard should actuate the individual man in all the relations of life. Take, for instance, the mission of the clergy, the profession of a lawyer, a physician, the calling of a tradesman, and indeed any other occupation, whether mental, artistic, physical, or manual, where each one's peculiar talent is called into requisition. Let us now apply our test to their several employments.

First, with the advocate or lawyer: we find that all in that profession, who, by the common consent of the Bar, are admitted to hold the first rank, scarcely ever disagree in pecuniary matters, because their talents enable them to judge correctly of the pecuniary value of the service of those engaged in their line of employment with the nicest precision. They know the time and the money, the wearisome days and sleepless nights, the anxiety of mind that must necessarily have been expended in the acquisition of that knowledge which has been called into requisition, and which forms, if we may so express it, the foundation-stone of his capital. They can judge correctly the amount of industry, the continued mental application necessary to render that capital available; the many days, months, and years, that have passed in perfecting that particular talent by which he has at length gained celebrity, whether as a skilful attorney, a special pleader, or a discreet counsellor. Knowing all this, they are enabled to form, and always do form, where their personal interests alone are concerned, a very correct idea of the value of such services as may have been required to be performed. This judgment, moreover, is rarely ever questioned by him, who, with like facilities for forming an unbiassed opinion, has given his service without stipulating a price. It is upon this principle, in the courts of law and equity, where one advocate is supposed to have made extravagant charges for his counsel and advice, as well as in the management of the case, the judge or chancellor appoints some discreet, conscientious and honorable man learned in the profession of the law, to tax the bill of costs.

Now, that which is done in this last resort, the honest advocate will do in the first place: he will not take advantage of the simplicity or kind-heartedness of his client, to filch from him that which he deliberately knows he has not fairly and honestly earned. Nor will he give his client an opinion that he knows to be legally unsound, for the express purpose of creating a business for himself, thereby wasting not only the time of him who depended on him for honest advice, but leading him blind-folded, as it were, into a mass of expenses that may cause his ruin. If he does, then we must rank him as the pettifogger, the cheat, and the swindler, in very truth—as that person who, whenever he looks into a glass, beholds the resemblance of a dishonored and dishonorable man.

As with the lawyers, so with all other professions and trades; the buyer and seller in their relative positions, considering honest dealing a commandment kept by the few, broken by the many, but revered by all.

Thus briefly have we introduced a subject of the greatest importance. The limits of this work will not admit of a more extended consideration of the subject, and the author is forced to content himself with these introductory remarks.

The foregoing pages are the result of the author's experience, covering nearly half a century, in this and other countries, and are sincerely offered to his fellow-citizens, particularly to the young, who have not yet entered the arena to fight the battle of life, and as a debt of gratitude to the system and institutions which enabled him, after landing on these shores a poor emigrant, to obtain a position of respectability and usefulness in the community which he delights to serve, and to promote whose interest it has been his honor to dedicate the best days in his life. "This great land, 'shadowing with wings,' is but just commencing to receive within its embrace the disfranchised millions of the older systems escaping thence to us, on the East and on the West. Commingled tongues and many creeds are fusing amicably together in this great interior receptacle of America, and the boy of to-day may live to see an empire arise from it strong enough to dictate the law of humanity to the world, and enlightened and noble enough in its policy to win the willing homage of all nations."

CHAPTER XXIV.

THE RELATION OF THE BUYER AND THE SELLER.

> "Lord Stafford mines for coal and salt,
> The Duke of Norfolk deals in malt,
> The Douglass in red herrings;
> And noble name and cultured land,
> Palace and park and vassal band,
> Are powerless to the notes of hand
> Of Rothschild or the Barrings."—HALLECK.

"NAPOLEON I. not inaptly called England a nation of shop-keepers." How far the great Emperor was right in his assertion, is, and will be, a disputed point, especially among Englishmen. The author of this work, for the present, declines the idea of offending, or defending, Mr. John Bull; for in either case the result would be a thankless task in the realm of fashion and dress. The French Emperor might have continued the sentence by saying, "perfide Albion" always takes care of number one, even at the expense of despoiling her more polite or weaker neighbors. Unfortunately for the happiness of the honest portion of mankind, the world contains at the present day too many individuals and nations, who, when tested by the scales of justice and impartial opinion, are nothing more nor less than legalized thieves, despoiling the honest man's peace and happiness. Having endeavored to show, in some of the preceding pages, the world's commendation of the honest man, in contradistinction to the villains who deal in false representations, weights and measures, and who by the corruption of wealth are protected by unjust laws;—the former is the hydra-headed monster, which must first be struck down to the earth, with all mental and bodily powers. Class legislation in favor of the few, and to suit unprincipled politicians, monopolists and others, in the mal-administration of existing good laws, are some of the many ills that the downtrodden, toiling masses are doomed to bear in this and other countries, until patriotic liberators, victorious heroes, shall arise; "first in peace, the first in war, and the first in the hearts of their countrymen," who will wage eternal and exterminating war against corruption and fraud in high and low places, by creating a powerful and invincible legion of patriots, creating an honest man's party, to wield the power of the pen in the first instance, or the sword as the last resort,* aided, if needs be, by good and patriotic people, assembling in their might, to use, as an auxiliary power, strong hemp rope, round the neck of incurable villains, who are false to the community; a short shrift and a hoist, dangling the evil-doers in the air higher than Haman.

* The pen is more powerful than the sword; we say the shears are more powerful than either or both; because the shears conquer woman, and woman is the mother of all mankind. What will a virtuous woman give to cover her nakedness? What will a bad woman do for fine dress? Answer ——

History repeats itself, " that necessity knows no law," and especially when it is of common occurrence for the unprincipled political judges who disgrace themselves, to the injury of our common country, by unscrupulously soiling the ermine of the judiciary, in allowing the worst species of criminals to go unwhipped of justice.

The reader will perceive by the foregoing remarks that the basis of all fair dealings commences at the root of impartial justice; and, like a mighty tree, its ramifications on earth are so multifarious that few people thoroughly understand the relative duties of each, as buyer and seller; the commonly received opinion that the party who receives a commodity is under no obligation to the deliverer on mutual settlement, and vice versa, thus rendering all interchanges in trade as entirely selfish, doing away with any friendly interest between each other. This mode of usage is entirely wrong; in proof, when a buyer and a seller receive each their respective considerations, this is the time to offer commercial civilities bordering on those of a social character. What can be more unreasonable than to suppose that a conscientious dealer has no other motive in serving the buyer with his best commodities, including his best services, unless he was acting under the belief that he is gaining your future patronage and friendship? Similar motives and a sense of duty ought to actuate the buyer in all honorable dealings, thereby rendering interchange of commodities of an agreeable and sincere character, performed in the courtesies that are usually practised in polite society.

It is hardly possible in the limits of this volume to give an idea of the incalculable pecuniary loss for the want of a proper foresight on the part of the buyer in guarding his his own actions from being made the basis of success by an expert counterfeiting knave, who assumes the role of a conscientious trader. The successful defrauder generally adopts the outside appearance and manner of business that well befits the high tone and character of the man of commercial integrity. He also too often finds any number of persons whom he can plunder, to a great or less extent, without using much wit or exertion in so doing, for the best of all reasons those victims are in the majority of cases previously prepared by the confidence of unwarrantable and inconsiderate practices adopted in commercial usages on the adage "you must first risk before you can gain."

How common it is in commercial dealings, and correspondingly in the social circle, to hear of the successful efforts of swindlers of every type, ingratiating themselves into the trust and confidence of their too confiding victims. The dealer's inordinate greed of gaining substance or renown are the chief resources of the designing knave; they are in very truth the deceiver's stock in trade; his tools whose leverage power in countless numbers of instances being the means of robbing the dealer out of the sweat of his brow, and the social circle out of many of their chief ornaments.

It may here be very properly asked, how can these losses and annoyances be in some way prevented, alleviated or avoided? This, indeed, is a question not easily or satisfactorily answered. It is so difficult to solve that, notwithstanding the author of these pages has been actively engaged in commercial life, commencing in the Old World as an orphan boy at the age of thirteen, graduating through all ranks of commerce and events, the observation of royalty and formulas of Republics, being for the last twenty odd years an adopted citizen of the United States of America, an agreeable exchange in lieu of my birth-right, a so-called British subject, the son of an Irish rebel, a gentleman of unsullied integrity, the latter in arms against that odious tyrant, George the Third.

The author, with a dear-bought commercial experience of over forty years, and not a stranger to the usages of well-regulated society, regrets his inability to correctly advise the unwary how to avoid the dark designs of the swindler, sharper, the thief, including deep-dyed villains of every type. Even ancient and modern history is so far unequal to the task. Therefore, all that can reasonably be expected from the author is to show the beacon lights of cosmopolitan experience, and the war of life's battle against the world's curse; an abomination of the Lord's—the dishonest man.

SUPPLEMENT.

SERIES FROM

EUROPEAN AND AMERICAN AUTHORS,

ON

DRESS AND FASHION, ANCIENT AND MODERN.

> Fashions that are now called new
> Have been worn by more than you:
> Elder times have used the same,
> Though these new ones get the name.
> MIDDLETON'S MAYOR OF QUEENSBOROUGH.

DRESS AND FASHION FROM ENGLISH AUTHORS.

DRESS, considered merely as a covering for the body, and as a means of promoting warmth, needs no explanation. In the early age, it was simple as the manners of the people who invented it. Leaves, feathers, and skins formed the clothing of our first parents. As civilization gradually spread over the world, and as the invention and genius of man found means to change a raw hide into leather, the wool of sheep into cloth, the web of a worm into silk, flax and cotton into linen; to extract from herbs, flowers, woods, minerals, and insects, dyes and colors that vie with the rainbow in richness and variety—they quitted the simple garments of their forefathers, and gradually gave themselves up to an almost incredible degree of luxury and extravagance in the adornment of their persons.* So extensively and so rapidly did this passion for dress spread over the world, that edicts, laws, and ordinances have been passed from time to time, by many nations, to arrest the growing evil; an evil created by that desire for personal distinction which dwells more or less in every human breast, whether male or female, and which marks the untaught savage of the Sandwich Islands as well as the enlightened and well-educated inhabitant of Britain. It may appear incredible to those who have not dived into the mysteries of dress and fashion, to learn that revolutions have been caused at different times, and among different nations, from the determined resistance opposed to the various laws and decrees which have been directed against the too great love of dress and ornament; and so powerfully has this passion exhibited itself in the human mind, that blood has actually been shed to support it.

In the history of China, we find that even that meek, quiet people were roused to fury when their Tartar conquerors ordered their luxuriant tresses to be cut off, and so strenuously did they oppose the arbitrary decree, that in more than one instance the unfortunate Chinese preferred losing their heads to parting with their beloved ringlets. We are also told that the Tartars waged a long and bloody war with the Persians, and declared them to be infidels, because they would not clip their whiskers after the fashion of the former.

Even so late as the eighteenth century, a very serious *émeute* took place in Madrid, on an attempt being made to banish the *capa* and sombrero; and, marvellous as it may seem, the obstinate resistance opposed to those who wished to change the fashion of those cherished articles of dress caused the disgrace and flight of the prime minister.

In our own country many laws and edicts have been made at different times to check, not only extravagance in dress itself, as regards the richness and splendor of its materials and ornaments that decorate it, but also to correct and regulate the shape of various parts of the apparel of both men and women. Several of our early kings waged war against the ridiculous and enormous length of piked shoes, and, by enacting a law restraining their points to a certain standard, hoped to correct the evil. But Fashion was not to be so ruled by the will of a monarch; angry at her wishes being disobeyed, she immediately put it into the heads of her followers to invent a mode equally absurd; the *crakowes* and *poulaines* disappeared, but were soon replaced by shoes of so extravagant a width, that another law was, ere long, found necessary to circumscribe their breadth.

Queen Elizabeth, though herself so devoted a follower of fashion, and so passionately fond of dress, still made many laws respecting the attire of her subjects. She commanded the lower orders to wear on the Sabbath-day a cap of a peculiar shape; and, perhaps to restrain the love of foreign fashions which had long been so prevalent in England, she enacted that this head-dress should be made of wool, knit, thicked, and dressed in Britain. She also made a decree to limit the size of the ruffs and swords worn by her courtiers to the standard she considered fitting for subjects to assume; and, fearful that so arbitrary a law might be in some way or other evaded by the votaries of fashion, she appointed officers whose sole duty it was to break every man's sword exceeding the limited length, and clip all the ruffs whose size infringed upon her legal ordinance.

Although the arbitrary laws caused some slight troubles at

first among gallants who could not brook the shortening of their cherished weapons, still no serious consequences ensued, and on the whole the English have ever borne the attacks made upon their dress with becoming *sang froid*. Elizabeth, too, busied herself in arranging the costume usually worn in the Inns of Court, and particularized the shapes and colors of the garments and the embroideries she considered befitting so grave an assembly.

Under Elizabeth's successor a serious debate took place in parliament, concerning the enormous size of verdingles; and some years afterwards laws were passed to put a stop to patching and painting.

The Turks, despotic in everything, will not allow the Grecian ladies the poor privilege of wearing petticoats of the length that fashion in their country has declared to be proper and fitting; they have officers whose duty it is to trim off as much of the jupe as ventures beyond the length fixed by their barbarous masters.

The Turks also have laws by which none but their own august persons are allowed to wear yellow slippers; and while their haughty brows were encircled with turbans of the finest and brightest-colored muslins, with silks of the richest dyes, or with shawls of the gayest tints and most delicate texture, their Grecian subjects were condemned to wear dark cotton caps, as a mark of their servitude; the Armenians, too, they oblige to appear in ridiculous-looking balloon-shaped cappas; and the crouching Jews look doubly miserable when forced to bend to the Turkish law, which only permits their heads to be covered with brimless caps, much resembling inverted flower-pots. These despots have however themselves been, within the last few years, constrained to bend to the decree of Sultan Mahmoud, who ordered that a red cloth fez, or military cap, should be worn by the followers of the faithful, instead of the lofty calpac or ample turban. This law was, however, received with the most determined and indignant remonstrances and opposition, and so obnoxious to the Turkish feelings was this new-fashioned head-dress, that the discontented party set fire to the houses of those who were favorable to the change; and though the Sultan's wishes passed into a law, his subjects are still highly disgusted with their forced adoption of any coiffure in the place of the turban so long worn by their forefathers.

Besides the many decrees made by our monarchs concerning dress, a particular costume was arranged by Charles the Second and his council, for the nobility to appear in, and one in which great extravagance of gold, silver, lace, and jewels was not necessary; for during his reign in England, the immense sums lavished upon dress and ornaments were almost incalculable.

Gustavus of Sweden also invented, or at least ordered a court habiliment, in which all who wished to be admitted to his presence, both men and women, were obliged to appear; and Bonaparte followed his example, to the no small disgust of his officers, and to the despair and anger of *les belles Françaises*. Even during the Revolution, when blood, murder, and misery, were spread over devoted France—when the prisons echoed with the groans of the unfortunate victims of political despotism—when the scaffolds were crowded with the dead and the dying—dress was not forgotten, and stormy were the debates on this important subject held in the national convention!

In various countries of Europe sumptuary laws have at different times been enacted, to restrain extravagance in apparels.

In Switzerland, Italy, and Germany, the legislature frequently found it necessary to interfere; and for this reason, probably, the national costume still remains in full force among the peasantry, who hitherto have resisted the approach of Fashion, and her handmaids, Caprice and Vanity. While on this subject, we must not forget to mention the peculiar privileges relating to dress belonging to the family of Andrea Dona. When, owing to the luxury and profusion which characterized the Genoese of his day, the senate found it absolutely necessary to check the growing evil, and forbade the wearing of jewels and brocade, the patriot admiral, doubtless to show his country's sense of the services he had rendered it, was allowed to expend what sums he pleased upon the adornment of his person; and this privilege was afterward extended to his family.

Woman is defined by an ancient writer to be an "animal

that delights in finery;" and it is to be feared the annals of dress in every land, the most savage as well as the most civilized, will but prove the truth of the assertion. Certain it is that the peacock, in all its pride, does not glitter in more various and gaudy trappings than does a modern woman of fashion. But while thus speaking of woman's love of finery, which appears from the most ancient writers to have belonged to her since the world began, we must not omit to mention that man also was, and in most countries still is, as much devoted to this passion as the fair sex. Though in these days, at least in most civilized nations, it is considered effeminate for men to adorn their persons with trinkets and embroidered garments, still those who peruse the "Book of Costume" will find that, however extravagant women have been in these respects, men have equalled, if not surpassed them in profusion and magnificence. Among savage nations, to this day, the warriors deck their persons with all the finery they can procure—with feathers, shells, beads and paint; while their wives are often obliged to content themselves with their blanket-covering, and but few ornaments.

In Exodus we read of the "jewels of silver, and jewels of gold," borrowed by the Israelites from the Egyptians. In Isaiah, also, we find a long account of female apparel in the time of the prophet.

Having thus pointed to our readers the antiquity of the toilet, we will speak of Fashion, who, "sole arbitress of dress," with the caprice for which she is so celebrated, has enacted, that what is the proper standard for attire in one country, and at one time, shall be equally the contrary in other climes, and at other periods.

Of all nations, the two that pay the most devoted attention to the decrees of fashion, in the size, shape, and color of every trifle relating to the toilet, are the English and French, and it seems a reflection worthy the consideration of the philosopher, why these two (we may truly say the most enlightened nations of the world) should, of all others, be the most determined and devoted followers of this feather and flower decked goddess.—*Annals of Fashion, London,* 1847.

DRESS AND FASHION—AMERICAN AUTHORS.

FASHION.

It was the ordinary remark of the fashionable Dr. Graham (in the days of Horace Walpole), when consulted by a patient, "Sir, your disease is very extraordinary, but it is common enough." This paradoxical definition may be very well applied as interpreting the word "Fashion." The latter is doubtless an extraordinary thing commonly adopted. It will seem still further paradoxical to assert that what is "fashionable" is "vulgar;" but when it is recollected that "vulgar" implies something popularly observed (the word being derived from "volk," "people"), the paradox is no longer apparent. The Latin terms *vulgus* and *vulgaris*, like our own translations of them, are not intended to convey anything complimentary in them. The designation *vulgus* was contemptuously flung at the ancient Germans by their Roman antagonists. The sons of Herman accepted the name, and the German "volk" soon became the fashionable or popular equivalent for "patriots."

In the term "mode" we have something of a similar meaning. It is derived from *mos*, a manner or custom. This word in its plural form, *mores*, signifies "morals," by which is meant manners, which, if not, ought to be in fashion. As in Latin the difference of number alters the signification, so in French does the change of gender. "Le moral," of a woman, is for instance, by no means the same thing as "sa morale." In deriving *mode* from "mos," we follow the lexicographer Boiste. We may add, however, that another Latin word, "modus," is not altogether to be set aside as the original of "mode." It implies a due proportion, neither more nor less; a just measure, or manner, and to be in the mode, according to this rendering of the original, is not to be extravagant—not to be in excess in anything. He who adopts *this* mode will find himself possessed of the most valuable of fashions—the true "*factu nobilum;*" although Livy had not the same application in his mind when he wrote the words just quoted.

The most ancient fashion with which we are acquainted is one which is just expiring. It commenced in Scythia, and is going out, after a long reign, in New Zealand. We allude to "tattooing." It is, or was, the offspring of some strange conceit on the part of the ladies. These latter were Scythians, who, holding in their power some Thracians of the same sex, amused themselves, says Clearchus, by tracing very ridiculous figures on their bodies by means of needles. The poor Thracian ladies, when restored to freedom, exercised their ingenuity by concealing the absurd figures etched on their bodies, in a labyrinth of flourishes, circles, and most perplexing patterns. The design was immediately adopted as fashionable wear, and every Thracian lady appeared in public tattooed from the head to the loins.

Since that period, the mode has been followed by various nations, and until very recently it was the characteristic of the New Zealand aristocracy. Of late years, however, the young chiefs look with something of contempt on their seniors so distinguished; and very speedily a tattooed skin will be as rare a thing in the isles of the Southern Ocean as perukes and patches, clouded caves and farthingales in the public promenades of England.

The fashions of the conqueror generally prevail over those of the conquered. Thus young British chieftains, despite the disgust of their sires, threw off their vesture of skins and put on the habits of their Roman victors. A consequence, only partially similar, followed the Norman invasion; the Norman cavaliers took from the Saxons their "smock-frocks," and with a change of material and an addition of ornament, introduced the blouse. When not engaged in military duties, the same invaders doffed their iron headpieces, and donned a wide-brimmed and easy covering of felt—this was nothing more than the modern "wide-awake." The *couvre-chef* of the lounging Norman has been stiffened into the peculiar head-gear of the Society of Friends; but its chief glory consists in its having been, in a modified shape and a scarlet hue, patronized by the Church of Rome, and fixed upon the brows of her humble cardinals.

Some one has defined "fashion" as being "the tyrant of fops and females." The definer might have added that the artificers in fashion's service are often the victims of fashion's slaves. There is nothing so powerful, so absolute, so imperious, and so transitory, as this same fashion. Napoleon himself was jealous even of this so-called goddess of fashion; and he condescended to sneer at her votaries, by saying that nations are sheep-like, and ready to follow the first who set a strange example. The simile is ricketty, and is not entirely correct. We have never heard of any one who followed the fashion set and advocated by Osclepiades, who tried to bring cheap locomotion into general favor, and who travelled about the world on a cow, living on her milk by the way. The above is an example set, which has never been followed. We may cite, on the other hand, a fashion followed, the originating example for which no one has yet discovered. We allude to "smoking." Of course, at this word, the thoughts naturally revert to Sir Walter Raleigh and Virginia tobacco. There were pipes, however, in our old monasteries, and the monks smoked "colt's foot" to keep the marsh air out of their stomachs. The fashion is probably of Eastern origin. That mention is not made thereof throughout the Arabian Nights, is no proof to the contrary; for we believe that in that picturesque series the undeniably prevalent Eastern fashion of opium-eating is not even alluded to.

* * * * * * *

Finally, reverting to "fashion" as simply in connection with dress, its past history reveals to us the counterfeit presentment of our ancestors; its present history, to be found in various contemporary authors, will convey a reflection of ourselves to those who will succeed us. It is a subject which unceasingly occupies the fool, and only passingly concerns the philosopher. Diogenes was not anything the more of a philosopher for living in a tub. He affected to fly the fashions of the day; but it has been truly remarked that while a fop is the slave of fashion, a philosopher surrenders himself to his tailor, whose duty lies in dressing him becomingly. He who entirely despises becomingness of attire, under an affected or an imaginary contempt for fashion, is as weak of head and mistaken in employment as he who sets all duties below the pleasure of watching the fashions and adopting them. These perish with daily perishing time, and, as the moralist of Dourdan sensibly remarks, " La vertu seule, si peu a la mode, va au-dela des temps."—*Encyclopedia Britannica, Boston, U. S.*

DRESS AND FASHION—AMERICAN AUTHORS.

COSTUME.

Costume (Fr. *costume*, custom), the style of dress characteristic of an individual, community, class, or age. So various and fickle are the modes of costume, that if the dressed man, and not the natural man, were the subject of science, and if men and women, like shells, minerals, flowers, and stars, were chiefly described and characterized by the way they strike the eye, rather than by more essential qualities, humanity would be the most complicated and perplexing branch of natural history. In an old poem, an English philosopher is represented as standing naked before a piece of cloth, with a pair of scissors in hand, trying in vain to decide in which of the various possible ways he shall clothe himself, and singing to himself:

"Now I will wear this, and now I will wear that,
And now I will wear I care not what."

Though no thinker has developed *a priori* the laws of costume, an observer of its phenomena in all ages would be able to reduce them to a few original types.

There are but two places naturally fitted to be the points

of support of the principal portions of dress: over the shoulders, and around the body above the hips. When attached by the shoulders, if no openings are made for the arms, or if the sleeves are so full and flowing as not to appear distinct from the principal garment, some one of the varieties of cloak is produced, as the chlamys, toga, peplum, palum, shawl, cassock, robe, cope, dalmatica, surplice, pelisse, mantle, and mantilla. If the garment is closer, so that the arms project through it, and have free play outside of it, some species of the tunic, various in length and quality, is produced, as the coat, waistcoat, frock coat, blouse, jacket, spencer, jerkin, doublet, super-tunic, surtout, gown, bodice, kirtle, chemise and shirt. Garments attached by the hips are distinguished into two classes, according as they envelop the legs, separately or together. Of the former class are all trouse, trousers, breeches, pantaloons, pantalettes, and drawers. Of the latter are the skirts or robes of gowns, aprons, and all the petticoats, as jupes, sous-jupes, joupons, kilts and farthingales. The peculiarities of different classes are often combined in the same garment, the skirt, which hangs from the waist, being united to a bodice, closely fitting the upper part of the body, and the lower garments being often suspended from the shoulders by straps. The coverings of the head, feet and hands are put on from the extremities, and are kept in place chiefly by being made close, though garters, shoe-buckles and strings, and occasionally straps, beneath the chin, are employed as fastenings; they include caps, hats, hoods, bonnets, turbans, tiaras, mitres, crowns, chaperons, cauls, cowls, plumes, crests, veils, wimples, headdresses (*coiffures*) commodes, chaplets, fillets, frontals, periwigs, perukes, ornamented combs, mufflers, stockings, hose, boots, greaves, buskins, thongs, shoes, slippers, moccasins, socks, gauntlets, gloves and mittens. The neck and wrists, and sometimes also the ankles, are regarded as natural sites for ornaments, such as collars, cravats, ties, gorgets, tippets, partlets, chains, bracelets, armlets and anklets. Tresses, ringlets, curls, ear-rings, finger-rings, watch-chains, and, rarely, nose jewels and tattooing make a part of costume. The junction of different portions is effected by brooches, clasps, pins, buckles, buttons and button-holes, hooks and eyes, cords, ribbons and knots.

Flowing garments are often brought close about the waist by a girdle, sash, belt, or zone. Every surface may be embroidered, furbelowed, flounced, trolloped, or puffed, and every border may be furnished with fringes, lappets, tags, aiglet, frills, ruffs, tassels, scollops, slashes, or various other styles of finish. Among the accessories of costume are the fan and cane. Leaves, feathers, and skins, which were the first material of clothing, have been succeeded by an immense array of cloths and furs, the result of an important industry in almost every part of the world, as various in texture and color as are the shape and purpose of the habiliments into which they are manufactured. In Egyptian and Hebrew history, the arts of weaving, dyeing, and embroidery were already in fashion. Egyptian workmen were clad with unrivalled simplicity, wearing generally only a short apron about the loins. They sometimes had also short drawers reaching half-way to the knee. The higher orders wore the same dress under an ample tunic of fine linen, reaching to the ankle, and provided with long sleeves. Only the outer and finer garments were worn by women. The priests usually wore the long robe of linen, of so fine texture as to be transparent, and over it a leopard-skin, as their costume of office. A wrapper was sometimes bound around the loose robe, covering the lower part of the body and falling in front below the knees; and while bearing the sacred emblems, the hierophants frequently wore a long full apron, tied in front with long bands, and supported by a strap over the shoulder. The head was also closely shaved, but sometimes covered with a wig, or tight cap. The texture of Egyptian linen, as proved by ancient representations, and by a piece recently discovered near Memphis, was equal to that of the finest now made. The Israelites were strictly commanded (Numb. xv. 38) to make fringes on the borders of their garments, adding a blue ribbon to the edge. A skirt or tunic to which a mantle was the outer covering, was their ordinary dress, and is still a frequent oriental costume. The Talmud enumerated eighteen garments which formed the clothing of the Jews from head to foot, among which are two sandals and two buskins. A figured girdle was worn around the waist, in which it was usual to carry a knife or poniard, which men of literary occupations replaced by an inkhorn. Bells and pomegranates on the bottom of the robe were ornaments peculiar to the high-priest. The dress of the women among the poorer classes seems to have consisted of loose trousers and a long gown; while women of superior condition wore over their linen dress a mantle resembling that of the men, but more closely fitting the person. The hair was worn long, braided with numerous tresses, trinkets, and ribbons; and the head-dress was adorned with jewels and pearls. Ear-rings and finger-rings were also fashionable; the eyelids and finger nails were stained, small mirrors were hung about the person as ornaments (as is still the custom of the Moorish women of Barbary); and a nose jewel was among the presents sent by Abraham to Rebecca. The dress of the Babylonians was a sort of flounced cylindrical robe, reaching from the neck to the feet. It appears sometimes on the monuments to consist of two garments, a short jacket, and an under-robe or petticoat, both alike flounced. The hair was worn long, and either fell in copious tresses or was confined by several varieties of head-dresses. The national costume of the ancient Persians was a close-fitting tunic and trousers of leather. The Median dress, on the contrary, was a loose flowing robe, which was applauded by Xenophon as concealing the form, and giving it an appearance of grandeur and elegance. A long frock, girdled with a cloak of thicker materials over it, was the dress of the early Greeks. The women were more closely robed in a tunic or shirt falling down to the feet, surrounded by an ample shawl or scarf, which not only enveloped the whole body, but sometimes covered the head or trailed upon the ground. Flowers were usually intertwined with their hair. The Tyrian purple and embroidery of the Sidonian women were in repute in the Homeric age. From the time of Pericles, the tunic was the principal article of female attire. It was made of linen, with sleeves covering only the upper part of the arm, and, being usually longer than the body, was drawn up and overlapped at the girdle, so as to reach only to the feet. Hence resulted the horizontal and undulating folds below the bosom, joined with the perpendicular folds of the skirt, which was a prominent characteristic of Greek drapery. All of the Greek outer garments were loosely attached, their chlamys, pallium, (himation) and peplum being properly translated scarf, blanket, and shawl. Unlike all the nations by which they were encircled, they wore nothing resembling pantaloons. The national and peculiar garment of the Romans was the toga. It was a full semicircular robe of white woollen, thrown freely about the body, flowing into many folds, and worn in different styles by every age and rank, that for priests and magistrates being bordered or striped with purple. The corresponding female dress was the stola, which was only an outer and more elegant tunic, reaching to the ankles or feet, furnished with sleeves, and having a flounce at the bottom. Under the flowing toga and stola were worn one or often two girdled and close tunics, which were larger and longer for the females. The Romans made their garments chiefly of linen and woollen, silk being unknown to them till after the close of the republic. There were celebrated Coan vestments made of muslin or gauze, so thin as hardly to conceal the form, and which were denominated by the satirists "woven wind." The Romans, like the Greeks, went with head uncovered, or with only a part of the toga drawn over it, when a cap, broad-brimmed hat (petasus), or helmet was worn. There were various coverings for the feet, those for the men being usually of black leather, those for the women white, or sometimes red, or yellow.

Early in the 14th century, fashions began to travel from Italy through Paris to London. At that period were introduced caps and hats of various fantastic shapes, plumes, and garments of more delicate texture, and the women began to ornament the borders of their shifts around the bosom and arms with needle-work. The female costume which appears in the painting of Giotto and his contemporaries is a robe or super-tunic flowing in folds to the feet, and coming high up in the neck, where it was met by the wimple of white linen. The sleeves terminated at the elbow in lappets, showing the sleeve of the under garment, which fitted the body tightly. The dress of the ancient Saxon, Norman, Scottish, and Danish women was a long girdled robe, and a full flowing mantle fastened on the breast. Sleeves and veils had become so long in the reign of Henry I. that they were tied up in bows and festoons. Great extravagance in dress prevailed in the reign of Edward III., when the men wore silk hoods, parti-colored coats with deep sleeves and narrow waists, short hose, long-pointed shoes, a bushy beard before and a tail of hair behind; and the ladies of distinction wore a turban or lofty mitre, with ribbons floating from it like streamers, a tunic half of one color and half of another, and a deeply embroidered zone, in front of which two daggers were suspended. "The ladies," says a poet of the period, "are like peacocks and magpies." The petticoat is first mentioned by this appellation in the 15th century, when it was worn by both sexes. Coat, or "cote," became a new name for a species of tunic about the same time. The kirtle, which is frequently alluded to in old romances, was the undergarment, white or more usually green, and sometimes laced close to the body like a bodice. Occasionally, in Anglo-Norman time, ladies in kirtle alone served in the hall; and at the close of the 15th century it was a habit of penance, and was worn as such by Jane Shore. In the reign of Queen Elizabeth, the Earl of Pembroke was the first who wore knit stockings in England, which were obtained from Mantua; and the Earl of Oxford brought also from Italy embroidered and perfumed gloves. The ladies wore farthingales and muffs of immense compass; and when the men introduced long swords and high ruffs, the jealous queen appointed officers to break every sword and clip every gentleman's ruff which was beyond a certain size. The breeches fell far short of the knees, the defect being supplied by long hose. The bodice of a lady's dress was made remarkably long. The fashionable hat had a broad brim and a high crown, diminishing conically upward. In the reign of James I. the cloak was more worn than it had been previously, and it continued to be in fashion after the restoration of Charles II. Silk garters puffed in a large knot were worn below the knees, and knots or roses adorned the shoes. Yellow starch for ruffs, invented by the French, was introduced in this reign by the example of a lady who soon after "went to be hanged in a ruff of that color." Long coats were worn by boys till they were about eight years of age, the present costume of the blue-coat boys of London being that of the time when Christ's Hospital was founded. After the restoration the periwig was introduced into England from France; and though preachers inveighed against it in their sermons, it soon became so much the reigning mode that a country gentleman is said to have employed a painter to place periwigs on the heads of several of Vandyke's portraits. In this reign the clerical habit assumed its present form; and it was also the era of shoe-buckles, open sleeves, pantaloons, and shoulder-knots. The ladies often wore green stockings patched and painted their faces in imitation of the French, and affected a mean between dress and nakedness which excited the reprehension of ecclesiastics. Pepy's "Diary" gives many minute details of the costume of this period. In the reign of William and Mary, Dryden complains that "our snippers (tailors) go over once a year into France to bring back the newest mode. The coat worn by gentlemen at this period was cut straight before, laced, and often buttoned in front, with large cuffs, but no collar. It was often fringed with gold and silver, and adorned with tassels. The breeches were close, reaching below the knee, the shirt was ruffled, the shoes were square-toed, and the hats were cocked. The peruke, of French origin, had expanded to an enormous size at the court of Louis XIV., and was copied in England, where it was worn alike by beaux, barristers, and the clergy.

* * * * * * *

Among the most important works treating of costume are the *Recherches sur les Costumes*, by Mailot (Paris, 1804); the collection *De Costumes, Armes, et Meubles*, by Viel Castel (Paris, 1828–33); the *Moden und Trachten*, by Hauff (Stuttgart, 1840); the *Trachten des Christlichen Mittelalters*, by Hefner (Frankfort, 1847, *et seq.*); the *Cootim Kunde*, by Weiss (Stuttgart, 1856, *et seq.*); the "Complete View of the Dress and Habits of the People of England, from the establishment of the Saxons in Britain" (London, 1796–99); and the very complete work of Ferrario on Ancient and Modern Costumes 2d edition), Florence, 1823–31.

American Encyclopedia, N. Y.

A STAR OF FASHION—ENGLISH BATH AND BEAU NASH.

* * * " Sent Hermes to Bath in the shape of a beau.
Long reign'd the great Nash, this omnipotent lord,
Respected by youth, and by parents adored;
For him not enough at a ball to preside—
The unwary and beautiful nymph he would guide;
Oft tell her a tale, how the credulous maid
By man, by perfidious man, is betrayed;
Taught charity's hand to relieve the distrest,
While tears have his tender compassion exprest.
But alas! he is gone! and the city can tell,
How in years and in glory lamented he fell."

"But whom have we here? Who is this? Right regally he approaches, right royal is he in his appointment. His six spanking grays whirl his chariot along in dashing style. How animated look his train, his out-riders, and the fellows clustered leg and wing behind his carriage! How enlivening the music of the band which accompanies him! how brilliant the tone of those horns, which startle the air with their clangour! How the people stop on every side to gaze on the *cortege* as it passes! How ladies and gentlemen of all degrees offer him courteous homage, which he as courteously acknowledges." * * *

This was the monarch of the eighteenth century, and an absolute monarch was he; his laws were like those of the Medes and Persians, unalterable; but it must be conceded to him that he never abused the "right divine." Survey we this monarch in his rule :—

Though Nash governed as if born to empire, the throne of Bath was not his by right: he had no hereditary claim; he was merely a citizen of the world; he was summoned by the voices of people to take upon his shoulders the sovereignty of Bath. He obeyed the call, and, like the King of the French, became the King of the People.

Like all the popular monarchs, King Nash was a strenuous advocate of reform, and Bath promoted it with all the influence of his potential voice, and enforced it with all the weight of his supreme authority. His first care was to improve the accommodations of his seat of empire. When he first undertook the government of Bath, it was a mean, dirty, and incommodious place; the lodgings for visitors were shabby, dirty and expensive; the public rooms were desecrated by all sorts of vulgarity and rudeness. Under the direction and authority of their new monarch, the corporation of Bath re-edified their city; and noble streets, beautiful squares, verdant gardens, soon combined their attractions. * * He drew up a code of ceremonial laws which he rigidly enforced, and which were implicitly submitted to by the inhabitants and visitors of the city.

Like all popular monarchs, he became very absolute. An

intimation of his royal will carried with it the form of a mandate with all the gentle sex; the other was often refractory. The King, however, was firm, and invariably, in the end, successful. Beau Nash had the unusual good fortune to be thrown by circumstances into the very position in which he was qualified to shine. The strictest etiquette was enforced, and the claims of precedence were rigidly adhered to. In the duead justment of these, Nash was unrivalled, and doubtless derived therefrom no small portion of the respect and deference with which he was uniformly treated; and a great addition was made to the comfort of the vast number of respectable middle classes who resorted to Bath, in the courteous treatment which the monarch of all exacted from them, from those titled individuals who had hitherto arrogated somewhat too much to themselves from the circumstance of their rank.

At this time the bath itself was the first fashionable resort in the morning, whither the ladies were conveyed in chairs, attired in their bathing-dresses, but with their heads dressed as if for an evening assembly; and while their bodies were receiving the benefit of the healing waters, their beaming countenances were turned to the surrounding gallery, whither the gentlemen duly repaired to pay their morning compliments to the fair. Soft music played around; and that no luxury might be wanting, no sense ungratified, each lady had a small floating-dish by her side, containing her pocket-handkerchief, nosegay and snuff-box. Could the gods in

Elysium have more?—Ye powers!—a finely-dressed head, a warm bath, a crowd of beaux, a band of music, a bunch of flowers, and a snuff-box!

Our readers need hardly be told that those were the days of minuets and country-dances. Quadrilles were unknown. Even the parent cotillion had not appeared. Gallopades were unheard of. Mazurkas were hidden in the womb of time. Polkas were an impossibility. And as to the exotic waltz, graceful though it be, young Englishwomen of those days, how wanting soever in some of the refining characteristics of these, had not learnt unblushingly to confide themselves to the arms of mere acquaintances of the other sex; to bear their close and not always respectful gaze; to feel their very breath on their necks, their cheeks, fanning the hair that strays on their face! Englishwomen can do this now; aye, and deem themselves modest; but—it is the fashion.

Amid a mass of frivolity and trifling, profusion and petty parade, many are the anecdotes recorded of Nash which would confer lustre on any man. He was a most shrewd and inveterate censor of slander and calumny; this qualification was an invaluable one to the Master of the Ceremonies at a fashionable and frivolous watering-place. His heart was most kind, his generosity great; and though himself a professed gamester, he was never weary in his endeavors to prevent the young and inexperienced from gaining the habit, or from being the dupes of another. To the young of both sexes, but to the fair especially, he was at all times a kind, a cautious, and a disinterested adviser; and the grave was not closer than himself, on any domestic secret committed to his keeping. * * * Nash's rule became absolute, and he was in acts and in reality what he was universally called —the King of Bath.

To the sick poor, who congregated at Bath for the benefit of its healing waters, he was a generous and unfailing benefactor; if not in his own person,—for he had seldom money to give,—by his personal exertions and his great influence with others. He was the main engine in the erection of an hospital free to the poor of all England, who required the Bath waters.

Surely this man should not descend to posterity as a mere beau—the peer only of Fielding and Brummell.—*Chronicles of Fashion, London,* 1845.

ESSAYS ON DRESS AND FASHION—1790-1868.

THE formalities of the 18th century received a severe blow, at the French Revolution; and in the ten years from 1790 to 1800, a more complete change was effected in dress, by the spontaneous action of the people, than had taken place at any previous period in a century. The change began in France, partly to mark a contempt for old court usages, and partly in imitation of certain classes of persons in England whose costume the French mistook for that of the nation generally. Thus new French dress was introduced by the party who were styled the Sans Culottes. It consisted of a round hat, a short coat, a light waistcoat, and pantaloons, a handkerchief was tied loosely round the neck, with the ends long, and hanging down, and showing the shirt-collar above; the hair was cut short, without powder, *à la Titus;* and the shoes were tied with strings.

The comparatively simple form of dress of the Sans Culottes found many admirers in England, and soon became common among young men; a change from the antique fashions was also greatly helped by the imposition of a tax on the use of hair-powder, which was henceforth usually abandoned. Pantaloons which fitted close to the legs remained in very common use by those persons who had adopted them, till about the year 1814, when the wearing of trousers, already introduced into the army, became fashionable. It is proper, however, to mention that trousers had, for the previous fifteen or twenty years, been used by boys and were perhaps from them adopted by the army. Previous to the French Revolution, the dress of boys was almost the same as that of men. Although trousers—called by the Americans pants—were generally worn after 1815, many elderly persons still held out in knee-breeches against all innovations; and of the present day, an aged gentleman may occasionally be seen clinging to this 18th century form of dress. The general use of white neckcloths continued, notwithstanding the introduction of the standing collar, till the reign of George IV., when this monarch's taste for wearing a black silk kerchief or stock, and also the use of black stocks in the army, caused a remarkably quick abandonment of white neckcloths, and the adoption of black instead. The year 1825, or thereabouts, was the era of this signal improvement in costume.

While these leading changes were effecting, other alterations of a less conspicuous nature were from time to time taking place. The disbanding of the army after the Peace of 1815, led to various transformations besides those we have mentioned. While pantaloons were the fashionable dress, it became customary to wear Hessian boots; these, which had originated among the Hessian troops, were without tops, and were worn with small silk tassels dangling from a cut in front, being drawn over the lower part of the pantaloons. They had a neat appearance; but the keeping of them clean formed a torment that prevented their universal use. * * When trousers were introduced from the practice of the army, the use of Wellington boots to go beneath them also became common. Referring to the era of 1815 to 1825, as that in which trousers, Wellington boots, and black neckcloths or stocks came into vogue, we may place the introduction of surtout in the same period of history. From the time when the collarless and broad-skirted coat had disappeared, about the commencement of the Century, the fashion of coats had changed in various ways till the above-named era, when the loose frock-coat or surtout was added to the list of garments.

Such is a general account of the progress of fashion in England, until nearly the present day. In these fashions, the Welsh, Irish, and Scotch have participated; and there is now little to distinguish the inhabitants of one part of the United Kingdom from another.

Some differences exist in particular localities, as, for instance, the round hats of the women in Wales, the checked gray plaid of the Lowland Scottish peasantry, and the kilts of the Highlanders. * * *

The general simplifying of dress subsequent to 1815 was not accompanied by an expiring effort to sustain a high style of fashion. The macaroni, or highly dressed beau of the 18th century, was succeeded by the dandy, who, with mincing, affected manners, prided himself on his starched collars, his trouser-straps, and the flashy bunch of seals which dangled from his watch-chain.

The Regency was the era of this kind of supreme dandyism, but it continued till later times, and characterized a number of leading public personages, of whom notices occur in "Raikes's Reminiscences" from 1831 to 1851. In the present day may be noted a kind of breakdown of everything like formality in gentlemen's walking costume; plain cloths, of divers hues, called tweeds have almost superseded materials of a superior quality. Cloth caps, or soft felted hats, called wide-awakes, cover the heads; and the feet are covered with short ankle boots instead of Wellingtons. In the evening or dinner costume, however, the old etiquette of dress coats and white neckcloths is still maintained. Among the changes that are taking place in the morning or walking dress, none is so remarkable as the growing fashion of wearing Knickerbockers.

These are wide loose trousers to below the knee, leaving the lower part of the leg only stockinged or covered with leggings. This fashion, which has been copied more immediately from the French Zouaves, and partly perhaps from the common practice of stuffing the lower parts of the trousers roughly into boots in the western regions of the United States, is very much a resumption of the costumes seen in old Dutch prints. Should it become general, leg-gaiters or boots will come again into use, and the present generation may live to see the fashion of male attire work once more round to the knee-breeches of the 18th century. In female as well as in male costume, fashion seems to have a tendency to work in a circle; of this the resumption of the farthingale or hoop, under the name of crinoline, * * * offers a sufficient example, besides affording a ludicrous instance of the unreasoning manner in which extravagances in dress are usually followed. It is to be observed, however, that Englishwomen, chargeable as they are with this absurdity, set a most creditable example to their sex all over the world, in allowing no fantastic change of fashion to prevent them from taking out-door exercise in all weathers, to which a recent introduction of India-rubber goloshes has materially aided.

As to the moral view that may be taken of the whimsicalities of female fashions, we might refer to the numerous papers of Steele, in the *Tatler* and *Spectator*, and also the writings of other 18th century essayists. Passing these over, it is enough to quote the words of Hazlitt, a more recent essayist. "Fashion," he says, "constantly begins and ends in two things it abhors most—singularity and vulgarity. It is the perpetual setting up, and then disowning a certain standard of taste, elegance, and refinement, which has no other formation or authority than that it is the prevailing distraction of the moment, which was yesterday ridiculous from its being new, and to-morrow it will be odious from its being common. It is one of the most slight and insignificant of all things. It cannot be lasting, for it depends on the constant change and shifting of its own harlequin disguises; it cannot be sterling, for, if it were, it could not depend on the breath of caprice; it must be superficial to produce its immediate effect on the gaping crowd, and frivolous to admit of its being assumed at pleasure, by the number of those who affect to be in fashion, to be distinguished from the rest of the world. It is not anything in itself, nor the sign of anything, but the folly and vanity of those who rely upon it as their greatest pride and ornament. It takes the firmest hold of weak, flimsy, and narrow minds; of those whose emptiness conceives of nothing excellent but what is thought so by others. That which is good for anything is the better for being widely diffused. But fashion is the abortive issue of vain ostentation and exclusive egotism; it is haughty, trifling, affected, servile, despotic, mean and ambitious, precise and fantastical, all in a breath; tied to no rule, and bound to conform to every rule of the minute." For a large variety of amusing particulars concerning fashions, with stars of fashion, etc., during the past two centuries, we refer to Mrs. Stone's Chronicles of Fashion (Lond. 2 vols. 1845).—*Chambers's Encylopedia*, 1868.

FASHION AND ITS LEADERS.

"A STORY," says an eminent writer, "is never too old to tell, if it be made to sound new." If this be true, I may be excused for relating the following veritable history:—

In an Indian jungle there once resided a tawny jackal, a member, as all those animals are, of a jackal club, which met at night in the said jungle. It was the custom for the different subscribers to separate early in the evening on predatory excursions; and on one occasion, the individual in question having dined very sparingly that day on a leg of horse, ventured, in hopes of a supper, within the precincts of a neighboring town. It happened that while employed in the prowling distinctive of his kind, he fell into a sunken vat filled with indigo, and when he had contrived to struggle out again, discovered, by the light of the moon, that his coat had assumed a brilliant blue tinge. In vain he rolled himself on the grass; in vain rubbed his sides against the bushes of the jungle, to which he speedily returned. The blue stuck to him; and so, with the acuteness with which jackals are renowned, he determined to "stick to" it.

Shame, indeed, would have overcome him, ridicule have driven him to despair, when he rejoined his club, but for this resolution. That very morning he appeared among his kind, whisking his tail with glee, and holding his head erect. A titter, of course, welcomed him, and before long you would have thought that every jackal present had been turned into a laughing hyena. Our hero was nothing abashed. "Gentlemen," said he, in the dialect of Hindustan, peculiar to his kind, "I have been to town, and bring you the last new fashion." The laughter changed to respectful admiration. One by one, the members of the club stole up to him, and inquired where he had met with the coloring, just as George IV. asked Brummell what tailor had made that coat. The address was imparted, and if on the following evening, not all of the prowling beasts appeared in a blue coat, it was only because three of them had been drowned in the attempt to procure it.—*Habits of Good Society*, N. Y., 1869.

Dress and sin came in together, and have kept good fellowship ever since. If we could doubt, as some have done, the authenticity of the Pentateuch, we should have to admit that its author was at least the shrewdest observer of mankind, inasmuch as he makes a love of dress the first consequences of the fall. That it really was so, we can be certain from the fact that it has always accompanied an absence of goodness. The best dressers of every age have always been the worst men and women. We do not pretend that the converse is true, and that the best people always dressed the worst. Plato was at once a beau and a philosopher, and Descartes was the former before he aspired to be the latter. But the love of dress, take it as you will, can only arise from one of two closely-allied sins, vanity and pride; and when in excess, as in the miserable *beaux* of different ages, it becomes as ridiculous in a man as the glee of a South Sea Islander over a handful of worthless glass beads. No life can be more contemptible than one of which the Helicon is a tailor's shop, and its paradise the park; no man more truly wretched than he whose mind is only a mirror of his body, and whose soul can fly no higher than a hat or a necktie; who strangles ambition with a yard-measure, and suffocates glory in a book. But this puny peacockism always brings its own punishment. The fop ruins himself by his vanity, and ends a sloven, like Goodman, first a well-dressed student of Cambridge, then an actor, then a highwayman, who was at last reduced to share a shirt with a fellow-fool, and had to keep his room on the days when the other wore it.

* * * "To be well dressed is to be dressed precisely as the occasion, place, weather, your height, figure, position, age—and remember it—your means, require. It is to be clothed without peculiarity, pretension, or eccentricity; without violent colors, elaborate ornament, or senseless fashions, introduced often by tailors for their own profit. Good dressing is to wear as little jewelry as possible, to be scrupulously neat, clean and fresh, and to carry your clothes as if you did not give them a thought."—*Ibid.*

OF THE BEAUTY OF COLORS.

The greatest part of colors are connected with a kind of established imagery in our minds, and are considered as expressive of many very pleasing and affecting qualities.

These associations may perhaps be included in the following enumeration: 1st, Such as arise from the nature of the objects thus permanently colored. 2dly, such as arise from some analogy between certain colors, and certain dispositions of mind; and, 3dly, such as arise from accidental connections, whether national or particular.

1. When we have been accustomed to see any object capable of exciting emotion, distinguished by some fixed or permanent color, we are apt to extend to the color the qualities of the object thus colored; and to feel from it, when separated, some degree of the same emotion, which is properly excited by the object itself. Instances of this kind are are within every person's observation. White, as it is the color of day, is expressive to us of the cheerfulness or gaiety which the return of day brings. Black is the color of darkness, and is expressive of gloom and melancholy. The color of

the heavens, in serene weather, is blue; blue is therefore expressive to us of somewhat of the same pleasing and temperate character. Green is the color of the earth in spring; it is consequently expressive to us of some of those delightful images which we associate with the season. The colors of the vegetables and minerals acquire, in the same manner, a kind of character, from the character of the species which they distinguish. The expression of those colors, which are signs of particular passions in the human countenance, and which, from this connection, derive their effect, everyone is acquainted with. 2. There are many colors which derive expression from some analogy we discover between them and certain affections of the human mind. Soft or strong, mild or bold, gay or gloomy, cheerful or solemn, etc., are terms obviously metaphorical, and the use, which indicates their connection with particular qualities of the mind. In the same manner, different degrees or shades of the same color have similar character, as strong, or temperate or gentle, etc. In consequence of this association, which is in truth so strong that it is to be found among all mankind, such colors derive a character from this semblance, and produce in our minds some faint degree of the same emotion, which the qualities they express are fitted to produce. 3. Many colors acquire character from accidental association. Purple, for instance, has acquired a character of dignity, from its accidental connection with the dress of kings. The colors of ermine have a similar character, from the same cause. The colors in every country which distinguish the dress of magistrates, judges, etc., acquire dignity in the same manner. Scarlet, in this country, as the color which distinguishes the dress of the army, has, in some measure, a character correspondent to its employment, and it was perhaps this association, though unknown to himself, that induced the blind man, mentioned by Mr. Locke, to liken his notion of scarlet to the sound of a trumpet. Every person will, in the same manner, probably recollect the particular colors which are pleasing to him, from their having been worn by people whom he loved, or from some other accidental association. In these several ways, colors become significant to us of many interesting or affecting qualities, and excite in us some degree of the emotions which such qualities in themselves are fitted to produce. Whether some colors may not of themselves produce agreeable sensations, and others disagreeable sensations, I am not anxious to dispute; but whatever colors are felt, as producing the emotion of beauty, that it is by means of their expression, and not from any original fitness in the colors themselves to produce this effect, may perhaps be obvious.

FORM, EXPRESSION, ATTITUDE.

It is very easy to see that the most different forms of feature are actually beautiful, and that their beauty uniformly arises from the expressions of which they are significant to us. The open forehead is expressive to us of candor and generosity, and suits a countenance which has that expression. The low forehead, on the contrary, is expressive to us of thought, of gloom, or melancholy. It becomes, therefore, a different expression of countenance. The full and blooming cheek suits the countenance of youth and mirth, and female lovliness; the sunken and faded cheek, the face of sensibility or grief, or of penitence; the raised lip, the elevated brow, the rapid motion of the eye, are all the concomitants of joyous beauty. The reverse of all these—the depressed lip, the contracted eyebrow, the slow and languid motion of the eye—are the circumstances which we expect and require in the countenance of sorrow or of sensibility. Change any of the conformations, give to the open and candid countenance the low forehead, to the face of grief the fresh and blooming cheek of joy, to the mourner the raised lip, or the elevated eyebrow, which are expressive to us of cheerful or joyous passions, and the picture becomes a monster, from which even the most vulgar taste would fly as from something unnatural and disgusting. If there were any real and original beauty in such conformations, nothing of this kind could happen; and however discordant were our emotions of beauty and of sentiment, we should still feel these conformations beautiful, just as we perceive, under all circumstances, colors to be permanently colors, or forms to be forms.

The slight illustrations which I have now offered, seems to me sufficient to convince those who will prosecute them, that there is no original beauty in any peculiar or distinct forms of the human features. There is another illustration which perhaps may still more strongly show the real origin of such beauty to consist in the expressions of which they are significant, viz.: That the same form of feature is beautiful or not, just as it is expressive or not of qualities of mind which are amiable or interesting to us. With regard to the permanent features, every one must have remarked, that the same form of feature which is beautiful in the one sex, is not beautiful in the other; that, as there is a different expression, there are different signs by which we expect them to be signified; and that, in consequence, the same signs are productive of very different emotions, when they are thus significant of improper or of unamiable expressions. They who are conversant in the productions of the fine arts, must have equally observed, that the forms and proportions of features which the sculptor and the painter have given to their works, are very different, according to the nature of the character they represent, and the emotion they wish to excite. The form of proportions of the features of Jove are different from those of Hercules; those of Apollo from those of Ganymede; those of the Faun from those of the Gladiator. In female beauty, the form and proportions in the features of Juno are very different from those of Venus; those of Minerva from those of Diana; those of Niobe from those of the Graces. All, however, are beautiful, because all are adapted with exquisite taste to the characters they wish the countenance to express. Let the theorist change them, and substitute for this varied and significant beauty the forms which he chooses to consider as solely beautiful, and the experiment will very soon show that the beauty of these forms is not original and independent, but relative and significant, and that, when they cease to be expressive of the character we expect, they cease in the same moment to be beautiful.

* * * * * * *

Of this second theory, therefore, " that there are certain relations or proportions of the different parts of the human form, which are originally and essentially beautiful, and from the perception of which all our sentiment of beauty in this respect arises "—it is, I trust, now unnecessary for me to enter into any lengthened refutation. Yet, as some opinions of this kind yet linger among connoisseurs and men of taste, and as the anxiety for some definite rules of judgment is ever more prevalent among such men than the desire of investigating their truth, it may not be unuseful to suggest the following very simple considerations, which every one of my intelligent readers must fully have anticipated.

If there were any definite proportions of the parts of the human form, which, by the constitution of our nature, were solely and essentially beautiful, it must inevitably have followed, that the beauty of these proportions must have been as positively and definitely settled as the relations of justice or of geometry.

To take an original sense for granted, and at the same time to suppose that the indications of this sense are variable, or contradictory, is a solecism in reasoning which no man will venture to support. If such a sense is supposed, then the universal opinion of mankind ought to be found to agree in some precise and definite proportion of the parts of the human form. If the opinions of mankind do not agree in such certain and definite proportion, then no peculiar sense can be supposed to exist, by which these sentiments are received.

That not only the sentiments of mankind do not agree upon this subject, but that the sentiments of the same individual differ in a most material manner, is a truth very susceptible of illustration. There is no form, perhaps, in nature which admits of such variety, both in appearance and proportion of parts, as the body of man, and which, therefore, seems so little capable of being reduced to any definite system of proportion. The proportions of the form of the infant are different from those of youth; these again, from those of manhood; and these again, perhaps, still more from those of old age and decay. If there were any instinctive sense of beauty in form in this long history, there would be one age only in which this sense could be gratified. Yet every one knows, not only that each of these periods is susceptible of beautiful form, but, what is much more, that the actual beauty in every period consists in the preservation of the proportions peculiar to that period, and that these differ in every article almost from those that are beautiful in other periods of the life of the same individual. The same observation is yet still more obvious with regard to the difference of sex. In every part of the form, the proportions which are beautiful in the two sexes are different, and the application of the proportions of the one to the form of the other is everywhere felt as painful and disgusting. If, however, there were any original and essential beauty in some definite proportion of parts, such effects could never happen. This definite proportion in every case would be solely beautiful, and every variation from it would affect us as a deviation or opposition to the genuine form of beauty. It may be observed in the same manner, that if the beauty of form consisted in any original proportion, the productions of the fine arts would everywhere have testified it; and that in the works of the statuary and the painter, we should have found only this sole and sacred system of proportion.

The fact, however, is (and every one knows), that in such productions, no such rule is observed; that there is no one proportion of parts which belongs to the most beautiful productions of these arts; that the proportions of the Apollo, for instance, are different from those of the Hercules; the Antinoüs, from the Gladiator, etc.; and that there are not, in the whole catalogue of ancient statues, two, perhaps, of which the proportions are the same. Against the hypothesis of an instinctive beauty in proportion, no fact can be so decisive as this. If there were any original beauty in peculiar proportions of the human form, the artists of antiquity must have perceived it when it was so easy a matter to ascertain it only by the labor of measurement and calculation; and that their productions are independent of such definite proportions, and that their effect is still produced, amid all this variation of proportion, are irrefragable proofs not only that the beauty of their works is not dependent upon such a theory of proportion, but that it arises from some higher causes and from some more profound attention to those feelings of human nature in which the sentiment of beauty is to be found.

If there were any original beauty in certain proportions of the human form (independent of all other considerations), then it must necessarily follow, that the same proportions of that form would, in all cases, be beautiful, and that all other proportions would affect us with sentiments of pain or of displeasure. If such a theory were maintained, let the philosopher state with accuracy the proportions that are thus instinctively beautiful. Let him then examine whether this doctrine corresponds with the most obvious facts in nature. The various ages of man are in some cases, and in all cases may be made beautiful by the genius of the painter or statuary. Are the rules of proportion applicable to all these cases? and do we admire the form of the child, the youth, the man, and the aged man, because they retain, amid all their changes, the same proportions? Is the beauty of the female form demonstrable only because it contains the same proportions with that of man? and is everything that deviates from the male proportion a blemish and a deviation from beauty in the female? These are obvious considerations. The pursuit of them, however, will lead every one that is capable of observation to still more satisfactory conclusion. If it is still further supposed, in aid of this infant theory, that there are certain proportions in sex, and in the various ages of human life, which are originally beautiful, it will not be easily supposed or maintained that there are similar instincts correspondent to the casual occupations of mankind, and that in every age, in the progress of society, and into every society which civilized man is formed, new or accidental instincts must be given, by which alone he can perceive the beauty of the forms around him. Yet all this must be supposed before, upon these principles, it is possible to account for the sentiments we every day feel, and for the illustrations which the artist every day gives us, with regard to the beauty of proportion. We see every day around us some forms of our species which affect us with sentiments of beauty. In our own sex, we see the forms of the legislator, the man of rank, the general, the man of science, the private soldier, the sailor, the laborer, the beggar, etc. In the other sex we see the forms of the matron, the widow, the young woman, the nurse, the domestic servant, etc. Is it by the principle of proportion alone, that in all these cases our sentiment of beauty is determined? Are the proportions the same in all these cases? Is not, in fact, our sentiment of beauty determined by the difference of these proportions; and would not the application of the same principles to each, destroy altogether the characteristic beauty which we expect and look for in such different cases? It is obviously the same in the arts of imitation. We expect different proportions of form from the painter, in his representation of a warrior and of a shepherd, of a senator and of a peasant, of a wrestler and of a boatman, of a savage and of a man of cultivated manners. We expect, in the same manner, from the statuary, very different proportions in the forms of Jove and of Apollo, of Hercules and of Antinoüs, of a Grace and of Andromache, of a Bachanal and of Minerva, etc.

The same attitude of gaiety which we feel as beautiful in the young, we should feel as disgraceful in the mature. The same gesture of joy which we should approve in the thoughtful and the old, we should consider as tame and unfeeling in the young. The grief of a young woman we expect to be expressed by greater violence of gesture than we should approve in a character of matron firmness; and the calm and subdued gesture of matron grief would, in the same manner, be painful or unsatisfactory to us in the form of the former. In pursuing this observation, it will be found that not only age, but profession, occupation, character of form, character of countenance, and a thousand other circumstances, determine our sentiments of the beauty of attitude or gesture, by determining the nature of the expression we expect from the individual we contemplate; and that the same gesture is beautiful or otherwise, precisely as it accords, or does not accord with the character we attribute to the form.

The severe and thoughtful gravity we admire in the attitude of a judge, would be absurd in a young lawyer. The step of dignity, the attitude of command which we love in the general of an army, would be ludicrous in a subaltern officer, etc. The same gestures or attitudes which we feel as beautiful or sublime in tragic imitation upon the stage, would be ludicrous, if they were employed even in the higher comedy, nor would they even be permitted by good taste in the inferior and less interesting characters of tragedy. It is unnecessary to say that the most approved or fascinating gestures of comedy would be altogether insufferable if they were employed in tragic representations. I shall only further request my readers to call to their remembrance the attitudes and gestures which they have so often admired in classic sculpture, and to ask themselves, whether the same gestures, etc., would be beautiful in all characters (as would necessarily be the case if beauty in this respect arose from any definite conformations); whether the gestures of the Apollo would be beautiful in the Hercules or in the Jupiter; or the attitudes of the Venus beautiful in the forms of Juno or Minerva? Even in the lowest employment of the art of painting (in portrait painting), we feel the necessity of this correspondence of attitude to character; and we blame the painter whenever he chooses any attitude or position which appears to us inconsistent with the character of mind which is expressed by the countenance. In feeling and in expressing, on the contrary, this correspondence, in selecting the attitude or gesture which suits best with the character he represents, consists one of the chief evidences of the genius of the artist; and by this means the portrait of an obscure individual may sometimes possess the value of an original composition.

The conclusion, therefore, in which I wish to rest is, *that the beauty and sublimity which is felt in the various appearances of matter, are finally to be ascribed to their expression of mind; or to their being, either directly or indirectly, the signs of those qualities of mind which are fitted, by the constitution of our nature, to affect us with pleasing or interesting emotion.*

ARCHIBALD ALLISON, LL. B., F. R. S., London.

"The best physical discipline is to be found in regular and cheerful exercises in the open air. Those sports which are often termed manly—but are not less womanly—as riding, boating, ball-playing, and brisk walking, are the best means of not only giving strength to the body, but enduing it with grace of form and motion.

"Such is the intimate relation between the body and mind, that it is impossible to do any good to either, unless the actions of both are kept in harmony. This truth is well demonstrated by the utter uselessness of all physical exercise for health's sake, and, we may say, for beauty's sake too, unless accompanied by a wholesome mental activity. Let any one, while depressed in mind, test his muscular power, and he will soon find how little able and disposed he is to use it. On the other hand, if he exerts his physical strength when under animating influence of pleasurable emotions, he is scarcely conscious of effort. If physical exercise is persisted in with the indisposition and incapacity for it that come from mental depression, the result is an excessive prostration, which is, of course, injurious to the health of the body. On the contrary, the exertion of the muscular force, stimulated and supported by a cheerful mind, can be continued almost indefinitely, with the good effect of giving increased vigor to the whole human system."

Book of Decorum.

DRESS AND FASHION.

LORD CHESTERFIELD TO HIS SON.—SENTENCES AND MAXIMS. REVISED BY C. A. SAINTE BEUVE, DE L'ACADEMIE FRANCAISE.

MONTESQUIEU, after the publication of "L'Esprit des Lois," wrote to the Abbé de Guasco, who was then in England—"Tell my Lord Chesterfield that nothing is so flattering to me as his approbation; but that, though he is reading my work for the third time, he will only be in a better position to point out to me what wants correcting and rectifying in it; nothing could be more instructive to me than his observations and his critique." It was Chesterfield, who, speaking to Montesquieu, one day, of the readiness of the French for revolutions, and their impatience at slow reforms, spoke this sentence, which is a resumé of our whole history: "You French know how to make barricades, but you never raise barriers."

Chesterfield had already said, more than twenty years previously, writing to the younger Crebillon, a singular correspondent and a singular confidant in point of morality,—Voltaire was under consideration, on account of his tragedy of

"Mahomet" and the daring ideas it contained,—" What I do not pardon him for, and that which is not deserving of pardon in him," wrote Chesterfield to Crebillon, " is his desire to propagate a doctrine as pernicious to domestic society, as contrary to the common religion of all countries. I strongly doubt whether it is permissible for a man to write against the worship and belief of his country, even if he be fully persuaded of its error, on account of the trouble and disorder it might cause; but I am sure that it is in no wise allowable to attack the foundations of true morality, and to break necessary bonds which are already too weak to keep men in the path of duty."

And it is precisely this sacred fire, this lightning that makes the Achilles, the Alexanders, and the Cæsars, to be the first in every undertaking, this motto of noble hearts, and of eminent men of all kinds, that nature had primarily neglected to place in the honest but thoroughly mediocre soul of the younger Stanhope. "You appear to want," said his father, " that *vivida vis animi* which excites the majority of young men to please, to strive, and to out-do others." "When I was your age," he says again, "I should have been ashamed for another to know his lesson better, or to have been before me in a game, and I should have had no rest till I had regained the advantage."

"Human nature is the same all over the world; but its operations are so varied by education and custom that we ought to see it in all its aspects to get an intimate knowledge of it."

"Almost all men are born with every passion, to some extent, but there is hardly a man who has not a dominant passion to which the others are subordinate. Discover this governing passion in every individual; search into the recesses of his heart, and observe the different effects of the same passion in different people. And when you have found the master passion of a man, remember never to trust to him where that passion is concerned."

"If you wish particularly to gain the good graces and affection of certain people, men or women, try to discover their most striking merit, if they have one, and their dominant weakness,—for every one has his own—then do justice to the one, and a little more than justice to the other."

He warned his son from the beginning against the idea that the French are entirely frivolous. "The cold inhabitants of the North look upon the French as a frivolous people who sing, and whistle, and dance perpetually; this is very far from being the truth, though the army of fops seem to justify it. But these fops, ripened by age and experience, often turn into very able men." The ideal, according to him, would be to unite the merits of the two nations; but in this mixture he still seems to lean towards France. "I have said many times, and I really think, that a Frenchman who joins to a good foundation of virtue, learning, and good sense, the manners and politeness of his country, has attained the perfection of human nature." He unites sufficiently well in himself the advantages of the two nations, with one characteristic which belongs exclusively to his race—there is imagination even in his wit. Hamilton himself has this distinctive characteristic, and introduces it into French wit. Bacon, the great moralist, is almost a poet by expression. One cannot say so much of Lord Chesterfield; nevertheless, he has more imagination in his sallies and in the expression of his wit than one meets with in Saint Evremond and our acute moralists in general. He resembles his friend Montesquieu in this respect.

"Enjoy an honorable and happy old age, after having passed through the trials of life. Enjoy your wit and preserve the health of your body. Of the five senses with which we are provided, you have only one enfeebled, and Lord Huntingdon assures me that you have a good stomach, which is worth a pair of ears. It will be perhaps my place to decide which is the most sorrowful, to be deaf or blind, or have no digestion. I can judge of all these three conditions with a knowledge of the cause; but it is a long time since I ventured to decide upon trifles, least of all upon things so important. I confine myself to the belief that, if you have sun in the beautiful house that you have built, you will spend some tolerable moments; that is all we can hope for at our age. Cicero wrote a beautiful treatise upon old age, but he did not verify his words by deeds; his last years were very unhappy. You have lived longer and more happily than he did. You have had to do neither with perpetual dictators nor with triumvirs. Your lot has been and still is, one of the most desirable in that great lottery where good tickets are so scarce, and where the great prize of continual happiness has never been gained by any one. Your philosophy has never been upset by chimeras which have sometimes perplexed tolerably good brains. You have never been in any sense a charlatan, nor the dupe of charlatans, and that I reckon as a rare merit, which adds something to the shadow of happiness that we are allowed to taste of in this short life."

The Art of Speaking.—"You cannot but be convinced, that a man who speaks and writes with elegance and grace, who makes choice of good words, and adorns and embellishes the subject upon which he either speaks or writes, will persuade better, and succeed more easily in obtaining what he wishes, than a man who does not explain himself clearly, speaks his language ill, or makes use of low and vulgar expressions, and who has neither grace nor elegance in anything that he says. Now it is by rhetoric that the art of speaking eloquently is taught; and, though I cannot think of grounding you in it as yet, I would wish, however, to give you an idea of it suitable to your age."

Keep Your Word.—"I am sure you know that breaking of your word is a folly, a dishonor, and a crime. It is a folly, because nobody will trust you afterwards; and it is both a dishonor and a crime, truth being the first duty of religion and morality; and whoever has not truth cannot be supposed to have any one good quality, and must become the detestation of God and man. Therefore I expect from your truth and your honor, that you will do that which, independently of our promise, your own interest and ambition ought to incline you to do; that is, to excel in everything you undertake.

Inattention.—"There is no surer sign in the world, of a little, weak mind, than inattention. Whatever is worth doing at all is worth doing well; and nothing can be done well without attention. It is the sure answer of a fool when you ask him about anything that was said or done, where he was present, that 'truly he did not mind it.' And why did not the fool mind it? What had he else to do there, but to mind what was doing? A man of sense sees, hears, and retains everything that passes where he is. I desire I may never hear you talk of not minding, nor complain, as most fools do, of a treacherous memory. Mind not only what people say, but how they say it; and, if you have any sagacity, you may discover more truth by your eyes than your ears. People can say what they will, but they cannot look what they will, and their looks frequently discover what their words are calculated to conceal. The most material knowledge of all—I mean the knowledge of the world—is not to be acquired without great attention.

"*The Well-Bred Man* feels himself firm and easy in all companies; is modest without being bashful, and steady without being impudent; if he is a stranger, he observes, with care, the manners and ways of the people the most esteemed at that place, and conforms to them with complaisance. Instead of finding fault with the customs of that place, and telling the people that the English ones are a thousand times better (as my countrymen are very apt to do) he commends their table, their dress, their houses, and their manners, a little more, it may be, than he really thinks they deserve. But this degree of complaisance is neither criminal nor abject, and is but a small price to pay for the good will and affection of the people you converse with. As the generality of people are weak enough to be pleased with these little things, those who refuse to please them, so cheaply, are, in my mind, weaker than they.

Insults and Injuries.—" However frivolous a company may be, still, while you are among them, do not show them, by your inattention, that you think them so; but rather take their tone, and conform in some degree to their weakness, instead of manifesting your contempt for them. There is nothing that people bear more impatiently, or forgive less, than contempt; and an injury is much sooner forgotten than an insult.

Lying.—" I really know nothing more criminal, more mean, and more ridiculous, than lying. It is the production either of malice, cowardice, or vanity; and generally misses of its aim in every one of these views; for lies are always detected, sooner or later.

"If I tell a malicious lie, in order to affect any man's fortune or character, I may indeed injure him for some time; but I shall be sure to be the greatest sufferer myself at last; for as soon as ever I am detected (and detected I most certainly shall be), I am blasted for the infamous attempt; and whatever is said afterwards, to the disadvantage of that person, however true, passes for calumny. If I lie or equivocate, for it is the same thing, in order to excuse myself for something that I have said or done, and to avoid the danger or shame that I apprehend from it, I discover at once my fear, as well as my falsehood, and only increase, instead of avoiding the danger and the shame; I show myself to be the lowest and meanest of mankind, and am sure to be always treated as such. Fear, instead of avoiding, invites danger; for concealed cowards will insult known ones. If one has had the misfortune to be in the wrong, there is something noble in frankly owning it; it is the only way of atoning for it, and the only way of being forgiven. Equivocating, evading, shuffling, in order to remove a present danger or inconvenience, is something so mean, and betrays so much fear, that whoever practises them, always deserves to be, and often will be kicked. There is another sort of lies, inoffensive enough in themselves, but wonderfully ridiculous; I mean those lies which a mistaken vanity suggests—that defeat the very end for which they are calculated, and terminate in the humiliation and confusion of their author, who is sure to be detected. These are chiefly narratives and historical lies, all intended to do infinite honor to their author. He is always the hero of his own romances; he has been in dangers from which nobody but himself ever escaped; he has seen with his own eyes whatever other people have heard or read of; he has had more *bonnes fortunes* than ever he knew women; and has ridden more miles post, in one day, than ever courier went in two. He is soon discovered and as soon becomes the object of universal contempt and ridicule.

"Remember, then, as long as you live, that nothing but strict truth can carry you through the world, with either your conscience or your honor unwounded. It is not only your duty, but your interest; as a proof of which, you may always observe, that the greatest fools are the greatest liars. For my own part, I judge of every man's truth by his degree of understanding.

Action! Action!—"Remember the adage: do what you are about, be that what it will; it is either worth doing well or not at all. Whoever you are, have (as the low, vulgar expression is) your ears and your eyes about you. Listen to everything that is said, and see everything that is done. Observe the looks and countenances of those who speak, which is often a surer way of discovering the truth than from what they say."

Vulgar Scoffers.—" Religion is one of their favorite topics; it is all priestcraft, and an invention contrived and carried on by priests, of all religions, for their own power and profit. From this absurd and false principle flow the commonplace insipid jokes and insults upon the clergy.

"With these people, every priest of every religion is either a public or a concealed unbeliever, drunkard, and whoremaster, whereas I conceive that priests are extremely like other men, and neither the better nor the worse for wearing a gown or a surplice; but if they are different from other people, probably it is rather on the side of religion and morality, or at least decency, from their education and manner of life.

Advantage of Manners.—" Manners, though the last, and it may be the least ingredient of real merit, are, however, very far from being useless in its composition. They adorn and give an additional force and lustre to both virtue and knowledge. They prepare and smooth the way for the progress of both, and are, I fear, with the bulk of mankind, more engaging than either.

"Remember, then, the infinite advantage of manners; cultivate and improve your own to the utmost: good sense will suggest the great rules to you, good company will do the rest."

How to be Considerable.—" Upon the whole, if you have a mind to be considerable, and to shine hereafter, you must labor hard now. No quickness of parts, no vivacity, will do long or go far, without a solid fund of knowledge; and that fund of knowledge will amply repay all the pains that you can take in acquiring it. Reflect seriously, within yourself, upon all this, and ask yourself whether I can have any view but your interest in all that I recommend to you.

No one Contemptible.—" Be convinced that there are no persons so insignificant and inconsiderable, but may some time or other, and in some thing or other, have it in their power to be of use to you; which they certainly will not, if you have once shown them contempt.

Woman.—" As women are a considerable, or at least a pretty numerous part of company, and as their suffrages go a great way towards establishing a man's character, in the fashionable part of the world (which is of great importance to the fortune and figure he proposes to make in it), it is necessary to please them. I will, therefore, upon this subject, let you into certain arcana that will be very useful for you to know, but which you must, with the utmost care, conceal and never seem to know. Women, then, are only children of a larger growth; they have an entertaining tattle and sometimes wit, but for solid, reasoning good sense, I never in my life knew one that had it, or who reasoned or acted consequentially for four and twenty hours together.

" Some little passion or humor always breaks in upon their best resolutions. Their beauty neglected or controverted, their age increased, or their supposed understanding depreciated, instantly kindles their little passions, and overturns any system of consequential conduct, that in their most reasonable moments they might have been capable of forming. A man of sense only trifles with them, plays with them, humors and flatters them, as he does with a sprightly, forward child; but he neither consults them about, nor trusts them with serious matters; though he often makes them believe that he does both, which is the thing in the world that they are proud of, for they love mightily to be dabbling in business (which, by the way, they always spoil); and being justly distrustful that men in general look upon them in a trifling light, they almost adore that man who talks more seriously to them, and who seems to consult and trust them. I say, who seems—for weak men really do, but wise ones only seem to do it. No flattery is either too high or too low for them. They will greedily swallow the highest, and gratefully accept the lowest, and you may safely flatter any woman, from her understanding down to the exquisite taste of her fan. Women who are indisputably beautiful or indisputably ugly, are best flattered upon the score of their understandings; but those who are in a state of mediocrity are best flattered upon their beauty, or at least their graces, for every woman who is not absolutely ugly thinks herself handsome, but, not hearing often that she is so, is the more grateful and the more obliged to the few who tell her so; whereas a decided and conscious beauty looks upon the tribute paid to her beauty only as her due, but wants to shine and to be considered on the side of her understanding; and a woman who is ugly enough to know that she is so knows that she has got nothing left for it but her understanding, which is consequently (and probably in more senses than one) her weak side. But these are secrets which you must keep inviolably, if you would not, like Orpheus, be torn to pieces by the whole sex. On the contrary, a man who thinks of living in the great world must be gallant, polite and attentive to please the women. They have, from the weakness of men, more or less influence in all courts; they absolutely stamp every man's character in the *beau monde*, and make it either current or cry it down, and stop it in payments. It is, therefore, absolutely necessary to manage, please and flatter them; and never to discover the least mark of contempt, which is what they never forgive; but in this they are not singular, for it is the same with men, who will much sooner forgive an injustice than an insult.

Affectation.—"Any affectation whatsoever, in dress, implies, in my mind, a flaw in the understanding. Most of our young fellows, here, display some character or other by their dress; some affect the tremendous, and wear a great and fiercely cocked hat, an enormous sword, a short waistcoat and a black cravat. These I should be almost tempted to swear the peace against, in my own defence, if I were not convinced that they are but meek asses in lions' skins. Others go in brown frocks, leather breeches, great oaken cudgels in their hands, their hats uncocked, their hair unpowdered; and imitate grooms, stage-coachmen and country bumpkins so well in their outsides, that I do not make the least doubt of their resembling them equally in their insides. A man of sense carefully avoids any particular character in his dress; he is accurately clean for his own sake, but all the rest is for the other people's. He dresses as well, and in the same manner, as the people of sense and fashion of the place where he is. If he dresses better, as he thinks, that is, more than they, he is a fop; but if he dresses worse, he is unpardonably negligent; but of the two, I would rather have a young fellow too much than too little dressed; the excess on that side will wear off, with a little age and reflection; but if he is negligent at twenty, he will be a sloven at forty, and stink at fifty years old. Dress yourself fine, where others are fine, and plain where others are plain, but take care always that your clothes are well made and fit you, for otherwise they will give you a very awkward air. When you are once well dressed, for the day, think no more of it afterwards; and, without any stiffness for fear of discomposing that dress, let all your motions be as easy and natural as if you had no clothes on at all. So much for dress, which I maintain to be a thing of consequence in the polite world.

Temper.—" The principal of these things, is the mastery of one's temper, and that coolness of mind and serenity of countenance which hinder us from discovering, by words, actions, or even looks, those passions or sentiments by which we are inwardly moved or agitated; and the discovery of which gives cooler and abler people such infinite advantages over us, not only in great business, but in all the most common occurrences of life. A man who does not possess himself enough to hear disagreeable things, without visible marks of anger and change of countenance, or agreeable ones without sudden bursts of joy and expansion of countenance, is at the mercy of every artful knave, or pert coxcomb; the former will provoke or please you by design, to catch unguarded words or looks, by which he will easily decipher the secrets of your heart, of which you should keep the key yourself and trust it with no man living.

A Father's Object.—" Dear boy, from the time that you have had life, it has been the principal and favorite object of mine, to make you as perfect as the imperfections of human nature will allow. In this view, I have grudged no pains nor expense in your education, convinced that education, more than nature, is the cause of that great difference which we see in the characters of men. While you were a child, I endeavored to form your heart habitually to virtue and honor, before your understanding was capable of showing you their beauty and utility. Those principles, which you then got like your grammar rules only by rote, are now, I am pursuaded, fixed and confirmed by reason, and indeed they are so plain and clear, that they require but a very moderate degree of understanding, either to comprehend or practice them. Lord Shaftesbury says, very prettily, that he would be virtuous for his own sake, though nobody were to know it, as he would be clean for his own sake, though nobody were to see him. I have therefore, since you have had the use of your reason, never written to you upon those subjects. They speak best for themselves; and I should, now, just as soon think of warning you gravely not to fall into the dirt or the fire, as into dishonor or vice.

Learning and Politeness.—"I have often asserted, that the profoundest learning and the politest manners were by no means incompatible, though so seldom found united in the same person, and I have engaged myself to exhibit you as a proof of the truth of this assertion. Should you, instead of that, happen to disprove me, the concern indeed will be mine, but the loss will be yours. Lord Bolingbroke is a strong instance on my side of the question; he joins, to the deepest erudition, the most elegant politeness and good-breeding that ever any courtier and man of the world was adorned with. And Pope very justly called him all-accomplished St. John, with regard to his knowledge and his manners. He had, it is true, his faults, which proceeded from unbounded ambition and impetuous passions; but they have now subsided by age and experience; and I can wish you nothing better than to be what he is now, without being what he has been formerly. His address pre-engages, his eloquence persuades, and his knowledge informs all who approach him. Upon the whole, I do desire and insist that from after dinner till you go to bed, you make good-breeding, address, and manners your serious object and your only care. Without them, you will be nobody; with them, you may be anything.

Hampden a Lesson.—" Lord Clarendon, in his history, says of Mr. John Hampden, that he had a head to contrive, a tongue to persuade, and a hand to execute, any mischief. I shall not now enter into the justness of this character of Mr. Hampden, to whose brave stand against the illegal demand of ship-money we owe our present liberties, but I mention it to you as the character, which, with the alteration of one single word, good, instead of mischief, I would have you aspire to and use your utmost endeavors to deserve. The head to contrive, God must to a certain degree have given you; but it is in your own power greatly to improve it, by study, observation and reflection. As for the tongue to persuade, it wholly depends upon yourself; and without it the best head will contrive to very little purpose. The hand to execute depends likewise, in my opinion, in a great measure upon yourself. Serious reflection will always give courage in a good cause; and the courage arising from reflection is of a much superior nature to the animal and constitutional courage of a foot soldier. The former is steady and unshaken, where the *nodus* is *dignus vindice;* the latter is oftener improperly than properly exerted, but always brutally."

Moral Character.—" Your moral character must be not only pure, but, like Cæsar's wife, unsuspected. The least speck or blemish upon it is fatal. Nothing degrades and vilifies more, for it excites and unites detestation and contempt. There are, however, wretches in the world profligate enough to explode all notions of moral good and evil; to maintain that they are merely local, and depend entirely upon the customs and fashions of different countries: nay, there are still, if possible, more unaccountable wretches; I mean, those who affect to preach and propagate such absurd and infamous notions without believing them themselves. These are the devil's hypocrites. Avoid as much as possible the company of such people, who reflect a degree of discredit and infamy upon all who converse with them. But as you may sometimes, by accident, fall into such company, take great care that no complaisance, no good humor, no warmth of festal mirth, ever make you seem even to acquiesce, much less to approve or applaud, such infamous doctrines. On the other hand, do not debate nor enter into serious argument upon a subject so much below it, but content yourself with telling these apostles, that you know they are not serious; that you have a much better opinion of them than they would have you have; and that, you are very sure, they would not practice the doctrine they preach. But put your private mark upon them, and shun them for ever afterwards."

Necessary Accomplishments.—"I here subjoin a list of all those necessary, ornamental accomplishments (without which no man living can either please or rise in the world) which hitherto I fear you want, and which only require your care and attention to possess.

"To speak elegantly whatever language you speak in;

without which nobody will hear you with pleasure, and, consequently, you will speak to very little purpose.

"An agreeable and distinct elocution; without which nobody will hear you with patience; this everybody may acquire, who is not born with some imperfection in the organs of speech. You are not; and therefore it is wholly in your power. You need take much less pains for it than Demosthenes did.

"A distinguished politeness of manners and address; which common sense, observation, good company, and imitation, will infallibly give you, if you will accept of it.

"A genteel carriage, and graceful motions, with the air of a man of fashion. A good dancing-master, with some care on your part, and some imitation of those who excel, will soon bring this about.

"To be extremely clean in your person, and perfectly well dressed, according to the fashion, be that what it will. Your negligence of dress, while you were a schoolboy, was pardonable, but would not be so now.

"Upon the whole, take it for granted, that, without these accomplishments, all you know, and all you can do, will avail you very little. Adieu.

Aim High.—"Aim at perfection in everything, though in most things it is unattainable; however, they who aim at it, and persevere, will come much nearer it than those whose laziness and despondency make them give it up as unattainable. *Magnis tamen excidit ausis* is a degree of praise which will always attend a noble and shining temerity, and a much better sign in a young fellow, than *serpere humi tutus nimium timidusque procellæ*, for men as well as women."

THE EMIGRANT—THE ADOPTED CITIZEN OF THE UNITED STATES, &c.

"Good heav'n, what sorrows gloom'd that parting day,
That call'd them from their native walks away,
When the poor exiles ev'ry pleasure part,
Hang round the bowers and wish'd in vain
For like these beyond the western main,
And shuddering still to face the distant deep,
Returned and wept, and still returned to weep."
—GOLDSMITH'S DESERTED VILLAGE.

"Take heed what you say, sir! an hundred honest men? Why if there were so many in the city, 'twere enough to forfeit their city charter."
—SHIRLEY'S GAMESTER.

PERHAPS there is no previous chapter in this book that requires more study, and which is more difficult to define, than the one that heads this article. In the first place, the newly-arrived emigrant in the United States, as a general thing, is dissatisfied with the country he has left. The hardships of the voyage across the ocean, even in the most favorable time of the year, sorely tries the temper and disposition of the cabin passenger, and, in a tenfold degree, the steerage voyager, as the worst of all berths aboard-ship is of course the steerage. The dissatisfaction of the emigrant is heightened beyond comparison at the unfeeling, and oftentimes cruel usage that "the old country" (greenhorn) passenger has to endure, at the hands of the lower classes of the bad portion of the sovereign people of this Republic. Instead of giving a kindly greeting and welcome to the newly-landed stranger, his person and effects are looked upon as so much lawful plunder, and by the time he runs the gauntlet of the baggage smasher, bummers, thieves, dock runners, black-legs, gamblers, the emigrant boarding-house keepers, the swindling ticket agents, and bogus employment and exchange offices, and countless other harpies, who systematically defraud the luckless stranger, the greenhorn emigrant frequently finds himself, very shortly after landing, worse than nothing; jaded in spirits, fleeced of all money and worldly goods, thereby becoming a low, degraded pauper. The emigrant passes through this unhappy state of existence while living, or when dead is buried in some Potter's Field, unwept, unknown and uncared for. If the emigrant escapes these hardships and wishes to make this country his future home, he must carefully avoid the land pirates (generally his own countrymen) as he would a deadly pestilence. No matter how shrewd or courageous he was in the old country, he must get away with all speed from these infamous land-sharks. He will find oftentimes, when it is too late, that he has been victimized out of his last piece of money, by the specious pretences of the confidence and other swindling games of some scoundrels in disguise, who pass themselves off as the American friends to the emigrant. The latter miscreants are more to be dreaded than some unseen sunken rock, or the coast-wrecker, who holds out false signals or beacon lights to the storm-tossed mariner, in order that they may glut their desire for plunder when the vessel is wrecked.

The politician and fourth of July stump orators, when they wish to flatter the adopted citizen and obtain his vote, assert that every emigrant that lands in America is a gain of $1,000 to the country of his adoption, even if he has not a cent in his pocket. If this assertion be true, the Americans have a strange and very extravagant way of using and taking care of the emigrant, who lands on the American shore; for the vital statistics too plainly show the sickness and burial of tens of thousands of emigrants, mainly brought about by the brutal and unfeeling ill-usage on land and sea. It is therefore to be sincerely hoped that the Northern people who waged the most destructive civil war on record, desolating the sunny South to emancipate the black race, will with equal firmness make some laudable effort to save the lives and scanty property of the unfortunate emigrant white race, on the principles of impartial justice and equality before the law, "in the land of the free and the home of the brave." This is no exaggerated statement, but, on the contrary, is of a worse description than here described. Such scenes can be witnessed daily at any of the emigrant seaport landings of this Union. It is much to be deplored that up to the present time, no effective remedy appears to exist in summarily punishing the unconvicted criminals, who thrive and prosper in setting all law, human and divine, at defiance, by robbing and cheating the defenceless emigrant, including the widow and orphans. Notwithstanding it is universally acknowledged to be one of the most serious stigmas that disgrace this great country. Is it to be wondered that the effete aristocracy points the finger of scorn at the young and old democracy of the New World? How long this lamentable state of affairs will continue it is hard to state, from the fact that for many years past, our local and national legislators have been principally engaged in framing questionable laws to elevate the African race on the one hand, and levy tax upon tax, and pile obnoxious tariff upon tariff, on the principle of how much can we personally make, because the so-called sovereign people have no rights which we are bound to respect. "What do we care, so long as we can enjoy a good fat office, and the emoluments thereof, for the suffering, laboring classes, the high cost of living, the stagnation of commerce, the annihilation of American-built shipping, an irredeemable paper currency, huge national debt, the neglected laws that ought to protect the public, and swiftly punish defaulting government officials, and others who unblushingly defraud the government to the extent of untold millions of dollars?" The majority of our present law-makers will answer all these allegations by their acts, but not expressed in words: What do we care as long as the people are our subservient tools, who vote for us and allow us to enjoy office? How often do we hear the American of the patriotic class, to the manor born, exclaim, that the teachings of George Washington and the early revolutionary Fathers appear to be of no account nowadays. The adopted citizen of many years adds his voice in unison with the pure American sentiment—"Give me the country as I found it, not as it is." It being now the most oppressively taxed country in the world; articles of luxury bear the smallest amount of tax, while indispensable products in daily consumption by the hard-working community bear, beyond all odds, the larger share, in accordance with dishonorable legislation, favoring the rich at the expense of the poor. The unprincipled law-maker, who will sell his country for his country's gold, impliedly answers by his acts: What do we care about the sovereign people's rights so long as we can retain office, with its emoluments?

> "Why should the sacred character of virtue
> Shine on a villain's countenance? Ye powers!
> Why fixed you not a brand on treason's front,
> That we might know t' avoid perfidious monsters?"—DENNIS.

This dissertation may appear to the reader to be wandering from the title of this chapter. We say no, for, to use a vulgar phrase, it is simply letting the cat out of the bag by relating unpalatable truths, however unpleasant to the wily politician of an unscrupulous order, or, what may be better understood, radically striking at the root of evil that aims to cut out some of the many ulcers that grievously afflict the body politic of this magnificent yet shamefully misused country. The more enlightened emigrant will at once perceive that the latter portion of this chapter is not a divulgence from its title, but, on the contrary, important information for him by which to govern his course, if he intends to remain an adopted citizen of this country. Fortunately for the Americans, to the manor born, and their fellow-citizens by adoption, all the ills herein alluded to are of a transitory character, that can be remedied to a more or less degree by the unanimous uprising of the people, and doing their duty with the ballot in lieu of using the bullet. It is said the darkest hour is the one before the dawn.* It is hard work to bring daylight out of the darkness which appears to overspread this land, where exists so much corruption and fraud. In very truth, if ever sacred history repeats itself, the comparison, in the author's opinion, holds good where our blessed Saviour whipped the thieves and money-changers out of the Temple. A similar remedy of a more extended description is absolutely needed in this country, by banishing some of the well-known plunderers of the people's treasure.

We join our voice in unison with that of an adopted citizen soldier who fought many a hard contested battle in the Union army, and say, "Let us have peace—and less taxes."

---

* N. B. Form a new Political Honest Party, to be known and called the " Cosmopolitan Party."

It is a very common mistake for the newly-arrived emigrant to suppose that this is a land flowing with milk and honey, and that he will have little or no exertion to obtain the same. This is a delusion, for in nine cases out of ten he will have to work harder in this country than in the one he left. Another egregious mistake is apt to be made, that the manners, customs and dress of the country he has left are superior in pattern to those of his new acquaintances here. The sooner he obliterates these ideas the better. "When in Rome do as Rome does," is a good maxim to observe, so far as changing his personal attire to the fashion of the Americans.

A stupid error is frequently made by the new-comer, in hanging around, spending his time and money in large cities that do not want his presence, while the more sparsely populated parts of the Union are always in want of the services of the industrious emigrant, and probably at a higher reward than he could obtain in the country he left, or the over-crowded American cities.

The Commissioners of Emigration and the Commissioners of Charity and Correction, are twin Institutions, established for the benefit of the emigrant and the poor, but in reality so distorted and mismanaged that they are nothing more nor less than so many monopolizing political machines. The proper care of the poor emigrant, sick and insane, is quite a secondary consideration with them, and has become a very convenient hypocritical cloak, like many other public institutions, especially situated in the cities of New York, Albany, and the National Capitol, Washington, D. C.

The mismanagement of the public institutions referred to, too unaptly are in fact the direct cause which compel the emigrant and poor to subsist as "at the Emigration, Ward's Island," on the lowest description of rations, and which has debarred them under pretended economy. To such an extent of tyranny has this become, that miserable humanity frequently arises in revolt " against the powers that be." The aristocratic nabob commissioners, under the feigned name of benefactors of the poor, quickly put down, with the aid of the Metropolitan police force, the outbreak, punishing the mutineers for their audacity in demanding the just enforcement of laws and the proper expenditure of the people's money. A portion of these assertions can be substantiated by visiting and examining the internal working and system of the Castle Garden Emigrant Depot, the Office of Outdoor Relief, Third Avenue; Bellevue Hospital, Blackwell's Island Penitentiary, Lunatic Asylum, &c., Ward's, Randall's and Hart's Islands, and various institutions of charity and correction. These being a few of the many public institutions where the people's money is so lavishly misapplied in paying large salaries and *sub rosa* contracts, &c.

It is commonly remarked by distinguished foreigners, citizens, and others who have been invited and accepted the princely hospitalities of the city fathers, that the above institutions are evidently established for the benefit, profit and luxurious ease of the said commissioners and their political partisans.

The emigrant, pauper, and others, who have occasion to traverse this great continent, will find to their sorrow that many of the guardians of the poor are like the rich man of old (as described in Scripture), and that the supplicant for relief, like Lazarus, will only receive the crumbs that fall from the rich man's table; therefore let them not believe that they will meet many true friends. The conclusion will evidently be forced upon them that their best friend is money, aided by their working brains and toiling hands, being the natural gifts from God to the rich and poor alike.

The reader of the preceding pages, as a matter of course, will infer that the denunciatory remarks of corruption and fraud practised in high places, tyrannical oppression, and especially in the collection of taxes and the management of various institutions of a public character, are all of a qualified form, and can be easily abated by the voice and votes of the people—the whole country being ripe for a change in the administration of public affairs, the basis of the change to be fair dealing between man and man, in view of the corruption practised and unblushingly advocated by a few dare-devil spirits (not forgetting gold-gamblers, railroad and fraudulent stock speculators) who overawe and circumvent their better-meaning and more honest associates. It is to be hoped that this change will soon transpire for the sake of millions of people who now inhabit, and millions more who would flock in increased numbers to this country, and gladly become citizens in upholding the flag and the glorious institutions of our common country. When the emigrant has adopted the enterprising spirit of the Americans, and has concluded to make this Union his permanent home, carefully preparing his plans accordingly, he will find plenty of room for skill and energy in all the legitimate walks of life, provided he maintains the dignified character of being a steady, sober, law-abiding citizen. The native Americans are not unlike the aborigines, for neither race place a very high value on land as compared with the Europeans. It is not to be wondered at, considering the almost unlimited expanse of this vast continent. One of the most popular rules in this country is "When you are sure you are right go ahead; never give up the ship;" try until you succeed in selecting the most suitable and profitable occupation, and remember God assists those who assist themselves. An enterprising adopted citizen willingly devotes his attention and money to the purchase of real estate. Singular to relate, that when he once secures a settlement in his new home, he frequently astonishes the American natives at his marvellous success, and is looked upon by his admiring fellow-citizens as a wonderfully smart fellow, or, as the Irish jestingly say, "Now that I have got a pig and a cow, everybody says good-morrow." The adopted citizen, who probably never owned an inch of land in the old country, finds himself, after reasonable exertion, in the possession of fixed property, say, a house and lot, a farm, a mammoth store, or broad acres, comprising a lordly domain in the New World.

"Freedom of the press; freedom of person and protection of *habeas corpus*, and trial by juries impartially selected."—JEFFERSON.

Liberty! Charity! Correction! Oh! what numerous crimes and humbugs are committed in thy name. Our English cousins, and others of the Caucasian race, will perhaps be a little surprised to learn that in the City and State of New York there are two separate and distinct forms of laws, one that upholds the principles of the constitution, combined with the freedom, justice, and protection conferred by Magna Charta; the more modern law, surreptitiously enacted, abolishes the fundamental principles of both those laws, the latter so revered by the English, who are, if possible, outrivalled by the law-abiding classes of the Americans who love and revere both those famed laws.

Notwithstanding "to make odious laws more odious," is to enforce them, it is further asserted that the war is over, yet unlawful arbitrary arrests still continue. In proof, any contemptible scoundrel and evil-disposed villain can, in company with another of equal turpitude and atrociousness, go before various presiding magistrates and make complaint under sworn affidavits, and ask for a committal warrant to arrest his innocent victim, under the pretence that he is an habitual, confirmed drunkard; on the mere fact of an *ipse dixit* of the complainant, the law-abiding citizen is forcibly arrested, deprived of the possession of his liberty and property, and incarcerated in one of the Inebriate asylums of the State, there to remain at the pleasure of his unprincipled persecutors, in order that they may, in many instances during his absence, despoil him more or less of his worldly goods, &c. The prisoner, a victim of false imprisonment by means of false oaths, is not examined under these circumstances, by any committing magistrate, nor does he receive the common privileges accorded to the greatest criminal, or the one that is guilty of the smallest crime.

All these high-handed outrages are, we may say, perpetrated and abetted under the jurisdiction and knowledge of the Commissioners of Charity and Correction; while the generality of the people suppose they are administering impartial justice and Christian charity to their unfortunate fellow-mortals! To such an extent has this villainous tyranny become that oftentimes all communications are rigidly excluded from the prisoner, thereby preventing him from the assistance of friends, or the advice of counsel whose duty it is to cause a writ of *habeas corpus* to be served upon said Commissioners to bring their prisoner before a just magistrate for examination—a proceeding attended with considerable expense and loss of time to the falsely imprisoned, which frequently terminates in sickness and death of the unfortunate prisoner. "Facts are stubborn things," and it behooves the enlightened community to rigidly investigate and, if possible, do away with these untold villainies. The same maltreatment the alleged inebriate receives under a false oath, and the obtaining of a committal warrant, is also applicable to the sane and insane who are unceremoniously sent to any of the Insane Asylums that the interested persecutors may desire. In immuring the sane with the insane on the principles of the *letters de cachet*, in any of these modern Bastiles, according to the form of arbitrary laws, it is necessary that the certificate be signed by two honorable or unprincipled physicians, as the case may be, by the interested complainants, to suit their nefarious ends, by the absence and restraint of the kidnapped individual. Such are some of the expedients that are unfortunately resorted to as law in this free and enlightened country.

It is alleged that fashion is like a great tyrant who governs all. We therefore take the liberty of reproducing an early quotation of this work: "Wherever we *go*, whatever we *do*, whatever we are, Fashion holds the wand of power over us, more blandly, but not less imperiously than the sceptre of empire was swayed by the Cæsars." If this quotation is correct in principle, the author, viz., "COSMOPOLITAN THE FIRST," claims the prerogative to introduce any subject within his grasp and to delineate it by the power of the pen, aided by his professional sceptre, the shears, in cutting out passages from sacred, profane, and modern history.

It will be observed from the dissertation just given upon the Emigrant, that, philosophically speaking, are we all in this migratory world emigrants. What has been the foundation of any nation or communities of people, but emigrants? It is therefore of the highest importance in the advancement and well-being of all nations that the emigrant should be hospitably received and taken care of according to his usefulness and deserts, and not, as is the common usage, treated with cold indifference on his arrival in this country. Instead of trying to make him a useful member of society, he is more frequently treated as if he were a criminal. The emigrant has hardly recovered from the mortifications and sorrows that previously surrounded his path, when another pang, more severe than all previous ones, stabs his very heart—especially if he is the parent of a young family. He will wonder, with more than ordinary amazement, how quickly his children have received the poison, and followed the pernicious example and unfilial manner with which insolent portions of "Young America" too often treat their parents. In the composition of this work, the reader will always understand commendable exceptions offer a bright example to the civilized world, how the junior American loves, reveres, and delights in obeying the lawful commands of his parents. It is a singular fact, and probably, when more minutely studied by the emigrant, who has been brought up in the land of his birth to rigidly obey and revere his parents, the reverse is too often the case in this great Republic, whose fundamental doctrine is that "all men are born free and equal," a sentiment that is very laudable and noble in inspiration, but, unfortunately for the good intentions of the founders of this republican system, it is one of the rocks upon which rising generations too frequently split. Their love of independence is so abused that it unknowingly descends into the vilest impudence and ingratitude. It is therefore not to be wondered at that he is the first to hear the hiss of the serpent,

> "How sharper than a serpent's tooth it is
> To have a thankless child!"
> —*King Lear.*

or feel the scorpion's sting from the child, to its parent. "Shame! oh shame! where is thy blush?" To the refined mind and sensitive heart, what can be more distressing in attempting to realize the countless evils that this destructive cancer brings? It too frequently reverses and undermines the natural affections and benign principles of our nature; the disrespectful and undutiful conduct that many ignorant children, especially in this country, show their parents, oftentimes accompanied with the most unnatural, hard-hearted treatment, instead of being the natural support and protectors of their parents, they are often the first to do them a wrong, deride, and insolently scoff at their kind advice and lawful authority.

"Train up a child in the way he should go, and when he is old he will not depart from it."—Prov. 22: 6.

It is not to be wondered at, so long as the prevailing practice sanctions ignorant young America to disregard with indifference and contempt the teachings of their seniors, as being old fogy ideas, and unworthy of their notice and respect.

In support of the latter remarks, the writer quotes from a modern American author : *

"The great reason of the failure of a broad, glowing friendship between parents and children—a failure so deplorable in our homes—is the lack in their characters of of that wealth, nobleness, sweetness, patience, aspirations, which would irresistibly draw them to each other in natural honor, love, and joy. The only remedy for this unhappy failure is the cure of its unhappier cause. Whatever makes characters deep, rich, pure, and gentle in themselves, tends to make them pleasing to each other. It is absurd to suppose that many hateful and miserable souls will love each other simply because they are connected by ties of consanguinity, of interest or duty. Whatever makes us suffer, especially whatever injures our finer emotions—even a mother, a son, a father, a daughter, may become such an object, as is illustrated with melancholy frequency. But when parents and children possess those higher qualities of soul, which naturally give pleasure, create affection, and evoke homage; and when they are not separated, or too

* William Rounsville Alger.

much distracted in alien pursuits, a firm and ardent friendship must spring up between them.   *   *   *   *

"To honor one's parents is the first Scriptural commandment with promise. It is a habit which no one will ever regret. But, alas! how many a man, how many a woman, has knelt on the grave where father or mother lay mouldering, and has lamented, with burning tears of shame and sorrow, the disobedience, disrespect, unkindness, and neglect shown in earlier years. How have they longed to lift up the faded forms from their coffins, to reanimate them, and to have them again in their homes, that, by unwearied ministrations of tenderness, they might atone for the upbraiding past.

"'Mother! thou art mother still,
  Only the body dies;
Such love as bound thy heart to me,
  Death only purifies.'"

CORRESPONDENCE.

TRIBUTES FROM THE LIVING,

AND

MEMENTOES FROM THE DEPARTED.

CORRESPONDENCE.

Copied Verbatim from the Original Autographs

IN THE POSSESSION OF

GEORGE P. FOX.

LETTERS FROM THE LATE DANIEL WEBSTER.

ASTOR HOUSE, *May* 28, 1852.

DEAR SIR:

If my K'haban is done, I should be glad it might be sent to me this morning, as I need it for travelling, this warm weather.

I leave the city at 1 o'clock to-day.

    Yrs. respectfully,

        DANIEL WEBSTER.

GEO. P. FOX, ESQ.

BOSTON, *May* 22, 1852.

GEO. P. FOX, ESQ., New York:

Dear Sir,—I have received your letter of the 21st inst., in relation to my summer paletot. I shall be in New York in the course of next week, and will call as you suggest at your establishment, if I feel able, but I would prefer that you should send it to the Astor House on Tuesday forenoon.

    Yours, truly,

        DANIEL WEBSTER

WASHINGTON, *April* 30, 1852.

DEAR SIR:

The suit of clothes you were so kind as to send me, fitted admirably well. They are exceedingly handsomely made, of fine material, and are really elegant—too elegant, I fear, for me. The K'haban is a very nice article, and I like it much. I wish you to furnish me one of lighter material, and lighter color, and sleeves not so deep, for spring and summer use. I expect to be at the Astor House on Monday, and shall pass the afternoon there, and should be glad if you would send me a few patterns, gray, drab, or some other color, from which I can make a selection.

Yours, truly,

DANIEL WEBSTER.

GEORGE P. FOX, Esq., Merchant Tailor, New York.

WASHINGTON, *June* 8, 1852.

GEORGE. P. FOX, ESQ., New York:

Dear Sir,—I have received the K'haban, which you sent me a few days ago, and am much pleased with it. It is the most comfortable and easy-fitting summer garment that I have ever worn.

I am, Sir, your

Obed't. Serv't.,

DANIEL WEBSTER.

LETTERS FROM G. J. ABBOT, ESQ., THE PRIVATE SECRETARY TO THE LATE HONORABLE DANIEL WEBSTER.

WASHINGTON, D. C., *Nov.* 28, 1852.

DEAR SIR:

In reply to your note received a few days since, I have to inform you that Mr. Webster was interred in his best blue coat, being the one which he had received from your establishment, as I understood, a short time previous to his death.

Yours, very respectfully,

G. J. ABBOT.

GEORGE P. FOX, Esq., New York.

WASHINGTON, *Dec.* 3, 1852.

ERASTUS BROOKS, ESQ.:

My Dear Sir,—I enclose a letter to Mr. Fox, which I hope is satisfactory.

When Mr. Webster was writing his Historical Address, he received from Mr. Fox his card, handsomely engraved, on which was the figure of a fox running, and the motto "*faire sans dire.*" I was struck with the appearance of the card, and placed it in a conspicuous situation, so that it should attract Mr. Webster's attention. He was dictating to me one of his most carefully prepared passages, that on the 37th page. He was walking backwards and forwards, and had got as far as the words " long foresight," when he paused to consider how to complete the sentence. At that moment his eye fell on Mr. Fox's card. He took it up, looked attentively at it, and then added, in a loud tone, what follows on that page down to "dire," bursting at the same time into a loud, ringing laugh, remarked, " Thank Mr. Fox for that idea." When he received his K'haban, after trying it on and admiring its easy and genteel fit, I asked him if I should acknowledge the receipt of it. He said he would dictate the letter himself. I gave the pen to an attendant, and he dictated the three lines which afterwards appeared in Mr. Fox's advertisement. This letter afterwards became famous again by an article in the *Boston Courier* of October 18th or 20th, as the identical *Blatchford Letter*, to which I hope you will call Mr. Fox's attention.

Yours, truly,

G. J. ABBOT.

ERASTUS BROOKS, ESQ., Editor New York Express.

WASHINGTON, *June* 28, 1854.

G. P. FOX, ESQ.:

Dear Sir,—I enclose herewith a private note to our consul, Mr. Saunders, bespeaking for you his kindly services.

Yours, truly,

G. J. ABBOT.

Extract from Mr. Webster's Address before the New York Historical Society.

The following most eloquent extract is the one in which Mr. Webster in his celebrated address before the N. Y. Historical Society, Feb. 23d, 1852, introduced Mr. Fox's motto as above related:

"Let this day ever be remembered. It saw assembled from the several colonies, those great men whose names have come down to us and will descend to all posterity.

"Their proceedings are remarkable for simplicity, dignity, and unequaled ability. At that day, probably, there could have been convened on no part of this globe an equal number of men, possessing greater talents and ability, or animated by a higher or more patriotic motive. They were men, full of the spirit of the occasion, imbued deeply with the general sentiment of the country, of large comprehension, of long foresight, and of few words. They made no speeches for ostentation, they sat with closed doors, and their great maxim was '*faire sans dire.*'

"It is true, they only wrote; but the issuing of such writings, on such authority, and at such a crisis, was action,—high, decisive, national action. They knew the history of the past; they were alive to all the difficulties and all the duties of the present, and they acted from the first, as if the future were all open before them. Peyton Randolph was unanimously chosen President, and Charles Thompson was appointed Secretary. In such a constellation, it would be invidious to point out the bright particular stars. Let me only say, what none can consider injustice to others, that George Washington was one of the number."

The Dress in which Webster was Entombed.

Daniel Webster, like some other gifted men that have brightened the age they have lived in, was great in everything. He respected the opinions and the customs of his country and of his time, in all points that merited his observation. But he would never change materially his style of dress while he lived, nor would he allow it to be done after he was dead. He left special directions to have his body after decease clothed in the garments he used to wear in the Senate of the United States; and those who bent over his coffin recognized that mighty form, robed in the same vest and the same blue dress coat, with the velvet collar and gold-wove cloth buttons, that he had last worn when he sat at the head of his own table, and was diffusing joy and beneficence around the glad circle gathered there to enjoy his hospitality. Nearly all the celebrated tailors of the country sought the privilege, at some period of his life, of making for him something to wear; but no one seems to have suited his taste so perfectly as Mr. George P. Fox; for not long before he died, Mr. Webster had ordered from him this same chaste, but richly made blue dress coat, and it was his desire that he might wear it to his tomb. Mr. Fox has received many compliments for the matchless skill he displays in his art—and he has studied it as an art, like an artist; but the highest honor that has ever been paid to his genius as a costumer, was paid by the great departed statesman of Marshfield.—*New York paper.*

DEPOSITION OF GEORGE P. FOX, TAKEN BEFORE MAYOR TIEMANN, OF THE CITY OF NEW YORK.

City and County of New York, ss.

George P. Fox, being duly sworn, deposes and says, that the piece of cloth hereto annexed is part of the same piece from which deponent made a blue dress coat to order for the late Hon. Daniel Webster, on the 25th February, 1852; and deponent has been informed by letter, by G. J. Abbot, Esq., the Private Secretary of Mr. Webster, that the said coat was worn by Mr. Webster in his lifetime, together with a buff vest and black cassimere pantaloons, and in accordance with the request of Mr. Webster on his death-bed, he was buried in the said suit of clothes of deponent's manufacture as above set forth.

Sworn to before me, this 12th day of August, 1859.

DANIEL F. TIEMANN, Mayor.

Letters from Millard Fillmore, Ex-President of the United States.

Washington, *July* 3, 1851.

Sir:

On my return from a short trip to Virginia, I had the pleasure to receive your favor of the 17th June, together with a fine specimen of black cassimere, which you have kindly presented for my acceptance, and for which I beg to return my acknowledgments.

I should be very happy to avail myself of your kind offer to make me a pair of pantaloons, but the truth is, I have found it more difficult to procure a perfectly fitting pair of pantaloons than any other garment, and on that account I have no pair which I should be willing to send on as a pattern. My son, to whom I have shown your letter, desires me to say that his stays, when passing through New York, have generally been very short, but he hopes at some time to give you a call.

Yours truly,

MILLARD FILLMORE.

Geo. P. Fox, Esq., New York.

Washington, *July* 15, 1851.

Sir:

I am this morning in receipt of your favor of the 12th inst., and shall be pleased to comply with your request to retain the cassimere I received from you, until your next visit to Washington, that you may be enabled to make it up.

Very truly yours,

MILLARD FILLMORE.

George P. Fox, Esq., New York.

WASHINGTON, *Feb.* 4, 1853.

GEORGE P. FOX, Esq., Merchant Tailor, New York :

Sir,—As it is possible that I may go South instead of North, at the close of my administration, I should be pleased to receive the suit of clothes which you are to make for me, at your earliest convenience, that any defect may be remedied before I leave this city.

Respectfully yours,
MILLARD FILLMORE.

WASHINGTON, *Feb.* 8, 1853.

MR. GEO. P. FOX, New York:

Sir,—Your letter of the 5th came to hand this morning, and in reply to your suggestion I would say, that I should be happy to see yourself and your foreman at your earliest convenience, in reference to the fitting of the suit of clothes which you are to make for me.

I am

Respectfully yours,
MILLARD FILLMORE.

LETTERS FROM GENL. FRANKLIN PIERCE, EX-PRESIDENT OF THE UNITED STATES.

WASHINGTON, D. C., 18*th July*, 1853.

MY DEAR SIR :

The President found your note of the 9th inst. awaiting, with many others, his return from New York, and he desires me to express to you the extreme mortification he feels to learn that the reception of your tasteful suit of clothes, forwarded some months since, has not been acknowledged.

The garments were all admirably adapted to the figure, considering the circumstances under which they were made, and will not require any alteration.*

* Was measured and fitted by Mr. Fox, simply by the eye.

The President desires me to assure you that he appreciates the kindness and generosity which prompted so handsome a gift.

With high regard, I am,

Yr. friend and servant,

SIDNEY WEBSTER.

Geo. P. Fox, Esq., Merchant Tailor, Broadway,

New York City.

Washington, D. C., 17*th May*, 1854.

George P. Fox, Esq.:

Sir,—The President's coachman and footman are in need of box coats for *summer.* I wish you to send, *as early as possible,* coats suitable for them in material and size. The cloth should be wool, but as *thin* as a regard for strength and durability will allow. The color I wish to be more distinct and decided than that of the coats you made in the winter. It must be a *handsome blue*, not light blue, nor very dark, but a medium. As to size, they should be cut to wear without any other coats under them. The buttons to be plain black. The length of skirt, I suppose need not be much longer than an ordinary frock coat. Perhaps you may like to put pocket-flaps upon the hips, to give the coat a distinctive character as a box coat. It should be made of as thin goods as will bear the pulling on and off, which strong men always subject their garments to when in haste.

Also, you may send for them each a pair of pants of the same material, or perhaps thinner, if you can get it, of the same color. Send me bill, for the President, with goods.

Truly yours,

SIDNEY WEBSTER.

WASHINGTON, D. C., 19*th July*, 1855.

DEAR SIR:

I return the sample of the goods selected for the coat. Probably no suggestion concerning the style or make of the garments is necessary. As it is to be a *dress coat*, the style will be the same, I suppose, as a dress coat of cloth. As it is to be for summer wear, and of light goods, it should be made up as light as possible, consistent with neatness of fit to the person. Would not nice grass cloth, or very fine hair cloth, be the best for stiffening about the chest, instead of heavy cloth?

As to-day is Thursday, I hope you will be able to forward the coat by the middle of next week.

Truly, yours,

SIDNEY WEBSTER.

GEO. P. FOX, Esq., New York.

WASHINGTON, D. C., 21*st July*, 1853.

MY DEAR SIR:

The black overcoat, to which you refer, was a most excellent fit, considering the circumstances under which it was made, and is considered by the President a most appropriate and a tasteful garment.

If I can be of any further service to you in any way, you must not fail to command me. It will give me pleasure to serve you always.

With high regard,

Your friend and obed't. serv't.,

SIDNEY WEBSTER.

GEO. P. FOX, Esq., Merchant Tailor.

AN INCIDENT IN THE LIFE OF THE AUTHOR.

On the receipt of the above note, the late ever-to-be-lamented Senator James, of Rhode Island, a kind friend and customer of the author, the very embodiment of the fully formed, developed man, being present giving his order for clothes, in the author's establishment, No. 333 Broadway, we handed him the open letter, at the same time asking him for his opinion and verbal reply to its contents. [All must know the late senator, who unfortunately lost his life in the prime of manhood, by the explosion of an ordnance gun of his own invention.] He replied, "Why, Fox, your fortunes are made in advance; all that you have to do is to go on to Washington, D. C., and call upon the President, Franklin Pierce. Rest assured that whatever office, in his gift, and that you think yourself qualified to fill, you can obtain, including the emoluments and pay of the same."

The author replied, "My name is Fox, one that walks on two legs; but it seems to me that you take me to be a jackass. Do you think I would be such a fool as to accept any office in the gift of the people? Sir, I have a good office of my own, a good wife, and fine stalwart children, and a prosperous mercantile business. I, therefore, decline to subject myself to the loss of a permanent, profitable business, and risk being turned out of office on the incoming of the next unknown administration." And so we say up to the present time. Furthermore this deponent saith not.

Correspondence with the Hon. STEPHEN A. DOUGLAS.

WASHINGTON, D. C., *July* 31, 1852.

My dear Sir:

Herewith you will find a draft by Selden, Withers & Co., on the Bank of Commerce, in your favor, in full for your bill.

Respectfully, your obed't serv't,

S. A. DOUGLAS.

Mr. GEORGE P. FOX, New York.

P. S.—Please acknowledge receipt.

CORRESPONDENCE WITH THE NAVY DEPARTMENT.

NAVY DEPARTMENT, *June* 26, 1852.

SIR:

In reply to your letter of the 25th inst., addressed to the Chief Clerk of the Department, I have to inform you that the patterns referred to in the Uniform Regulations will probably be received in a few days, when a copy will be sent to you.

I am, respectfully,

Your obed't serv't,

WM. A. GRAHAM.

MR. GEORGE P. FOX,
    Broadway, New York.

CORRESPONDENCE WITH THE LATE COMMODORE MATHEW C. PERRY AND GEORGE P. FOX.

NAVY SCHOOL, ANNAPOLIS, MD.,
June 3, 1852.

DEAR SIR:—

If you have not yet put the lace on my coat and pantaloons, I will thank you not to do so until my return to New York, as I have some doubt whether it will not be better to use English imported lace.

Respectfully,

Your obed't serv't,

M. C. PERRY.

GEORGE P. FOX,
    Broadway, New York.

Will Mr. Brown, at the Naval Store-keeper's office at the Navy Yard, please give to Mr. Fox the name of the Contractor for blue flannel for the Navy?

M. C. PERRY.

Mr. Horseman:—

Please deliver to the bearer (Mr. G. P. Fox) my cap.

M. C. PERRY.

June 23d, 1852.

Mr. Gustavus A. Ratz:

Please deliver to Mr. George P. Fox, or his order, my new sword-belt and epaulets.

M. C. PERRY.

At Mr. Belmont's office,
 corner of Beaver and Hanover streets.

Correspondence with the Department of State.

Department of State, Washington,
October 2d, 1852.

Geo. P. Fox, Esq.,
 333 Broadway, N. Y.

Sir,—As requested in your note of the 29th ult., I send herein a description of the uniform for U. S. Consuls, recommended in the instructions from the Department. It is proper to state that it is not obligatory upon Consuls to adhere closely to the same, but they are left free to adopt such other dress as may be suited to the place of their respective residence. The Department has never caused any drawings to be made of a Consul's full dress, otherwise they should have accompanied the inclosed.

I am, Sir, respectfully,
 Your obed't serv't,
  C. M. CONRAD,
   Acting Secretary.

WASHINGTON, *January* 28, 1854.

DEAR SIR :—

I have been requested by Mr. G. P. Fox, a highly respectable person who is engaged in an extensive business in New York, as a merchant tailor, to address you a line in behalf of his son, who is about to visit Europe on matters connected with business, and to express the hope tha you may be able, without inconvenience, to facilitate the objects he has in view. I take occasion to inclose a Consular list corrected to date.

    I remain, sir,
     Very respectfully,
      Your obed't serv't,
       GEORGE I. ABBOT,
        Consular Bureau.

GEORGE N. SANDERS, Esq.,
 U. S. CONSUL, London, England.

LETTER OF THE HON. THOMAS CORWIN, INTRODUCING MR. GEO. P. FOX TO GEN'L. WINFIELD SCOTT.

      WASHINGTON, D. C., *Dec.* 22d, 1852.

DEAR GENERAL :—

This note will be presented to you by Geo. P. Fox, emperor of all the wide-world dominion of Tailordom. Mr. Fox furnishes all the clothing in vogue for civil and military gentlemen, and begs of me the favor of this note of introduction.
    Very truly yours,
       THOS. CORWIN.

MAJOR GEN'L. SCOTT.

CORRESPONDENCE WITH THE HON. EDWARD EVERETT.

It would be convenient to Mr. Everett to receive the garments ordered of Mr. Fox some weeks since.

WASHINGTON, *Feb.* 14, 1853.
MR. GEORGE P. FOX, Broadway, New York.

Correspondence with the Hon. HORACE GREELEY, Editor of the New York Tribune.

Mr. Fox:—

I did not receive your bill with my clothes. Please send it by bearer, and oblige

Yours,

HORACE GREELEY.

Geo. P. Fox, Broadway,
New York, *July* 7, 1854.

Letter from ROBERT BEALE, formerly Sergeant-at-Arms of the United States Senate.

Senate Chamber, *Feb.* 18, 1852.

Dear Sir:

I have seen a variety of specimens of the work of Mr. Fox, who bears this, and I take great pleasure in introducing him as a gentleman who stands at the head of his profession. He is very appropriately styled the Leader of Fashion. He is here for the purpose of getting orders from gentlemen who desire to have garments made fashionable, durable, and tasteful. I have given him an order for a suit for myself, which I was induced to do from examining the neatness, and, indeed, beauty of the mechanical execution of his work.

ROBERT BEALE,

To George P. Fox, Esq.,
333 Broadway, New York.

Senate Chamber, *March* 15, 1852.

My Dear Sir:—

I acknowledge with great pleasure the receipt of the suit you made for me; it suits me exactly; in point of material, quality, color, fit, finish, and neatness of execution nothing can be more perfect; they fit with all the ease of an old suit, while they exhibit all the polish of a new. I would not have the alteration of a hair in any one of the vestments, and I beg you to preserve my measure.

You will be good enough to make a summer suit at your convenience; the material, color, and, in short, all that appertains to them, I leave to your superior taste and judgment. A lady complimented you by saying my suit was neatly beautiful.

With my best wishes, I remain,

Your friend and obed't serv't,

ROBERT BEALE.

To GEORGE P. FOX, ESQ.,
333 Broadway, New York.

CORRESPONDENCE WITH THE HON. G. W. WRIGHT, EX-MEMBER OF CONGRESS FROM CALIFORNIA.

HOUSE OF REPS., WASHINGTON, D. C.,
December 4, 1850.

MY DEAR SIR:—

Please get me up a *bona fide* Navy blue dress coat, first quality, gilt buttons, and a pair of first quality black doeskin pants, and forward the same forthwith by Adams' Express.

Please send us a few of your cards.

Very respectfully,

G. W. WRIGHT.

MR. FOX, Merchant Tailor,
Broadway, N Y.

WILLARD'S HOTEL, WASHINGTON, D. C.,
January 22, 1853.

MY DEAR FOX:—

Your very kind favor of the 15th inst., under cover to Senator Gwin, was duly received, and would have received my immediate attention but for the fact that I was hourly expecting to hear from your city. My long delay, however, has only proven the necessity of a still longer stay, and I now write this line to inform you that I shall leave here either on Thursday or Friday next.

I shall avail myself of the pleasure of an immediate call upon you upon my arrival. I had but an hour or two while in New York last, and found it impossible to pay my respects to the Napoleon of America.

I have many things to say, and a few orders to be filled. I leave for California on the 20th of March, or the 5th of April; meantime, I trust I shall have the pleasure of presenting to you many of my friends who are bound to occupy prominent positions in the new administration, and of course we shall both feel great pride in seeing them dressed like gentlemen, to say the least.

Very respectfully,
Your devoted friend,
G. W. WRIGHT.

Geo. P. Fox,,
    Broadway, New York.

Extract of Presentation of the Speeches of T. F. Meagher Esq., the Distinguished Irish Orator to Geo. P. Fox.

Presented to G. P. Fox, Esq., by T. F. Meagher, in most friendly acknowledgment of the very handsome and costly gift he gave me the 10th of January, 1853, the anniversary of my escape from Van Dieman's Land; in acknowledgment, moreover, of his unvarying attention to me ever since my arrival in America, and with the heartiest wishes for his continued success in that profession which his honesty, patriotism, and great ability has adorned.

Letter from an Unknown Correspondent.

Dayton, Ohio, *Oct.* 11, 1852.

Mr. George P. Fox:—

Dear Sir—Inclosed you will find $50, for which I want you to make me, as soon as possible, an Oriental K'haban of black or blue. Make it to suit your own taste, except the sleeves, which I want in overcoat style. Direct to me, Burnet House, Cincinnati, care of John L. Cassiday.

Yours, &c.,
A. MASON.

LETTER FROM THE MOST REV. THEOBALD MATHEW, THE GREAT APOSTLE OF TEMPERANCE.

MY DEAR MR. FOX:—

Accept my sincere thanks for your exceeding generosity, in presenting me, unsolicited, with a superb suit of black cloth clothes. The delicate manner in which you conferred this favor much enhances the value of the gift.

      Believe me,
       Your grateful friend,
         THEOBALD MATHEW.

New York, *Oct.*, 25, 1851.

CORRESPONDENCE WITH JENNY LIND.

G. P. Fox will please take Miss Lind's instructions for making a gentleman's morning-wrapper, and oblige

         JNO. F. KING.

  (Countersigned)   JENNY LIND.

LETTER FROM SIR H. L. BULWER, FORMERLY AMBASSADOR FROM ENGLAND TO THE UNITED STATES, NOW HER BRITANNIC MAJESTY'S AMBASSADOR TO CONSTANTINOPLE.

SIR:—

I will call on you to-day, and there are a few small alterations in the trowsers which I will suggest.

      Yours very truly,
        H. L. BULWER.

GEO. P. FOX, ESQ., &c., &c., &c.

(A.)

LETTERS FROM B. LYTTON, THE SON OF SIR EDWARD BULWER LYTTON, BART., FORMERLY ATTACHE TO THE BRITISH LEGATION AT WASHINGTON, AND NOW CELEBRATED FOR HIS POETICAL REPUTATION AS "OWEN MEREDITH."

I beg to testify to Mr. Fox's ability as an artist of great genius both in the conception and execution of every work and branch of a profession of which he is rightly entitled "the President."

BULWER LYTTON.

BRITISH LEGATION, Washington,
February, 1852.

(B.)

BRITISH LEGATION, *Dec.* 5, '51.

DEAR SIR :—

As the 1st of January is approaching, and I shall be in want of my uniform on that day, I have availed myself of Mr. Moore, one of H. M. Messengers, being in New York, to request him to bring it with him on his return to Washington. I would, therefore, be obliged to you if you would give it to him or his order.

The waistcoat you sent me I received quite safely—it is not the exact color which I thought I had mentioned, but is very well made, and *fits* well.

※ ※ ※ ※ ※ ※ ※ ※

I should be glad to know if you think you are likely to be in Washington during the winter, as if I remain in this country the whole of that season, I shall be in want of some winter clothes, and would wait till I could see you before getting them, if you are likely to be here then.

I should also be glad if you would inform me, if you are not coming up here, I could send you the amount of your bill to New York.

Your obed't servant,

B. LYTTON.

TO GEOEGE P. FOX, ESQ.,
New York City.

LETTER FROM COL. SCOTT CUNNINGHAM, PAYMASTER U. S. N.

WASHINGTON, *Oct.* 8, 1862.

MY DEAR FOX:—

On Wednesday last, I visited the tomb of Washington, at Mount Vernon, and brought away a stick suitable for a walking cane, which I shall take pleasure in offering for your acceptance. The wood is yet in too green a state to admit of being mounted with head and ferrule. It should be allowed some months seasoning, and I shall therefore send it to you "in the rough," with all its hallowed associations. You are a patriot and will duly appreciate it.

I was delayed in getting to New York on the 1st. I shall probably leave here next Wednesday or so.

Thine truly,
JOHN SCOTT CUNNINGHAM.

GEO. P. FOX, Esq.,
333 Broadway, N. Y.

The cane above referred to has been beautifully mounted, and encased in the head, under a glass cover, is a piece of the identical uniform blue coat, and a piece of the buff cassimere of General Washington's vest and small clothes, in which he surrendered his commission at Annapolis, in 1783.

LETTER FROM THE GALLANT CAPT. BLAKE, U. S. NAVY.

Mr. Fox has made for me a uniform which has given me the most entire satisfaction. I can safely recommend him to the officers of the Navy.

GEORGE S. BLAKE, U. S. N.

NEW YORK, *2d Jan.*, 1857.
TO CAPTAIN HUDSON, *Steamer Niagara.*

LETTER FROM AN APPRECIATIVE VALUED FRIEND AND CUSTOMER.

JEFFERSON, CHEMUNG Co., *Jan.* 23*d*, 1852.

GEORGE P. FOX, Esq.:

Dear Sir,—I received the coat you sent me by express this morning. Also your letter and bill. I have just paid the bill ($40) to Mr. Richmond, express agent here, and you will doubtless receive the amount simultaneously with the letter.

I have now received all the articles of clothing I ordered, and it is with pleasure that I express myself not only satisfied, but highly gratified at the manner in which you have fulfilled my expectations. True, Mrs. Watkins may have aided in the selection of the goods, but I think, *it is only George P. Fox* who could have turned out articles made from these goods in such perfect taste and finished style. The coat is a neat, easy, and perfect fit; so with the other articles. Had I been personally present, and measured and re-measured, you could not have succeeded better.

It follows that you are sure of my patronage and good offices, so far as others are concerned. Though the patronage of one individual *is small*, yet it is *small parts* of which great and mighty wholes are composed. I shall probably be in the city in about a month, when I shall do myself the pleasure to make you a short call. Meantime I am truly yours, &c.

GEO. G. FREER.

FROM A FACETIOUS WESTERN FRIEND AND CUSTOMER.

We publish the following humorous correspondence (per U. S. mail) of an original description, between a well-known fashionable Broadway tailor and one of his admiring customers, now temporarily sojourning in one of the Western States, for the reader's amusement. The letters bespeak, in part, the spirit of the times. Some people, at all hazards, wish to dress, and will dress, becomingly. They get tired of "old clothes," notwithstanding the war, and the more dismal hue and cry of "hard times."

MADISON, WISCONSIN, *Jan.* 22d, 1862.

My Dear Sir,—I regret that I have kept you waiting for the enclosed draft. I have been in daily expectancy of seeing you soon in New York, and scarcely thought it worth while to send so small a sum, when it would do just as well to give it to you personally.

I would give you an order for some new editions of your "beautifying in cloth," but really anything does to wear out here in the West, and I'll reserve my new skin till the animal gets where civilization can gaze upon him and appreciate the genius of "Fox." Here the talent of ten thousand Foxes is lightly held in esteem. A fur cap, a rough coat, and a pair of moccasins, being as nearly as possible full dress.

May your store be thronged, your be purse full, and your prosperity be plenteous, throughout 1862, and on through the century.

Faithfully yours,

E. P. H * * * * * *.

To GEO. P. FOX, Esq., Architect in cloth,
824 Broadway, New York City.

---

824 BROADWAY, NEW YORK, *Jan.* 29, 1862.

My Dear Sir,—Your kind favor of the 22d inst. is to hand this day covering draft for the amount of your account to date, as per enclosed receipt, and for which please accept my most sincere thanks.

I cordially approve of your desire to give me an order for some new editions of beautifying clothes, on your return to civilized New York. A philosopher may attempt to write, but never could fully describe how dejected and miserable a refined disposition like yours must at present feel, whilst vegetating as you are, and moulting your feathers, and rusting out your existence, in that out of the way place, Wisconsin.

Only imagine E. P. H * * * * * * *, "a gentleman and scholar, the painter and sculptor by times," clad in a fur cap, a rough coat, and a pair of moccasins, and this is the only possible full dress in that unfashionable region of our land, the "far West." They say "fine feathers don't make fine birds," but rest assured, when Geo. P. Fox gets hold of the now animal E. P. H * * * * * * *'s rough outer skin, he will tear it to pieces with the voracity of a four-legged sly fox, and re-adorn the Apollo-like figure of E. P. H * * * * * * *, Esq., with "fine feathers," viz., a combination of fine broadcloth, with silk, satin, velvet, and net cassimere. There now, friend, is not this a "Roland for your Oliver?" Do not your facetious compliments pale before the effectual fire of my rejoinder?

I am yours respectfully, ever grateful and obliged,

G. P. F.

To E. P. H * * * * * * *, Esq. Briggs' Hotel,
  Chicago, Ill.

Letter from a Member of the French Legation at Washington, D. C.

Washington, le 17 *Fév.*, '52.

Mr. Geo. P. Fox:

Monsieur,—J'ai recu le pantalon que vous m'avez envoyé en justifiant parfaitement votre devise *Faire sans dire*. Malheureusement, il ne m'allait pas, ou qui n'a rien d'étonnant puisque vous ne m'avez jamais vu. Mon colligue de Richmond, M. Henri Tabouelle, le trouvant à son gout et à la taille l'a pris et m'a chargé de vous prier de lui envoyer le bill, *au Louis de la Legation de France.*

Je m'adresserai à vous avec plaisir à l'occasion. Agriez, Monsieur, l'assurance de ma parfait consideration.

L. DEJARDIN.

UNITED STATES OF AMERICA.

STATE OF NEW YORK.

City and County of New York, ss. :

BE IT REMEMBERED, That on the sixteenth day of October, in the year of our Lord one thousand eight hundred and fifty-six, GEORGE PATRICK FOX (late of Great Britain) appeared in the Court of Common Pleas, for the City and County of New York, the said Court being a Court of Record, having common law jurisdiction, and a clerk and seal, and applied to the said Court, to be admitted to become a CITIZEN OF THE UNITED STATES OF AMERICA, pursuant to the directions of the Act of Congress of the United States of America, entitled "an Act to establish an uniform rule of naturalization, and to repeal the Acts heretofore passed on that subject," passed April 14th, 1802 ; and the Act entitled "an Act for the regulation of seamen on board the public and private vessels of the United States," passed March 3d, 1813 ; and the "Act relative to evidences in case of naturalization," passed 22d March, 1816 ; and the Act entitled "an Act in further addition to an Act to establish an uniform rule of naturalization, and to repeal the Acts heretofore passed on that subject," passed May 26th, 1824 ; and an Act entitled "an Act to amend the Acts concerning naturalization," passed May 24th, 1828 ; and the said applicant, having thereupon produced to the Court such evidence, made such declaration and renunciation, and taking such oaths, as are by the said Acts required, THEREUPON, it was ordered by the said Court, that the said applicant be admitted, and he was accordingly admitted to be a CITIZEN OF THE UNITED STATES OF AMERICA.

In testimony whereof, the Seal of the said Court is hereto affixed, this sixteenth day of October, 1856, and the eightieth year of the Independence of the United States.

[Seal.]   By the Court.

BENJ. H. JARVIS, CLERK.

LETTERS FROM SIR JOHN F. CRAMPTON, FORMERLY BRITISH AMBASSADOR TO THE UNITED STATES, NOW H. B. MAJESTY'S AMBASSADOR TO ST. PETERSBURGH, RUSSIA.

WASHINGTON, *May* 5, 1852.

SIR :—

I inclose you a check for the amount of a bill against Mr. Lytton.

* * * * * * * * * * * * *

If you will be good enough to send me the receipt I will forward it to him.

Your obed't serv't,

JOHN F. CRAMPTON.

GEO. P. FOX, Esq.,
    New York.

WASHINGTON, *June* 16, 1852.

SIR :—

I inclose herewith a check for your bill. Please send me a receipt for the same.

Your most obed't serv't,

JOHN F. CRAMPTON.

G. P. Fox, Esq.,
    New York.

LETTER OF ISAAC V. FOWLER, ESQ., POSTMASTER OF NEW YORK.

POST OFFICE, NEW YORK,
March 16, 1859.

DEAR SIR :—

Permit me to introduce to you Mr. George P. Fox, of New Jersey, who wishes to see you on a matter of business connected with the department.

He is a gentleman of character and position, and you can implicitly rely upon the correctness of any statements made by him.

Very respectfully yours,

ISAAC V. FOWLER.

HORATIO KING, Esq.,
Assistant Postmaster-General,
    Washington, D. C.

CORRESPONDENCE WITH THE WAR DEPARTMENT.

ADJUTANT-GENERAL'S OFFICE,
WASHINGTON, *Feb.* 17, 1860.

SIR:—

Your letter of the 9th inst., to the Secretary of War, has been referred to this Office, and in partial compliance with your request, a copy of the Army Register for 1860 has been transmitted to your address.

A revised edition of the regulations respecting the dress of the army is now in preparation for the press. A copy will be furnished you at the earliest moment practicable.

Very respectfully,
Your obed't serv't,
S. COOPER.
Adjutant-General.

To GEO. P. FOX, Esq.,
No. 824 Broadway, N. Y.

LETTERS FROM MEMBERS OF THE FRENCH LEGATION AT WASHINGTON, D. C.

NEW YORK, LE 30 *Janv.*, 1862.

MON CHER AMI:

Mr. George P. Fox, tailleur fashionable de New York, m'a fait un uniforme, une habit de soirée et une Redingotte habillée à ma très grande satisfaction. Il a un coupeur francais, dont je fais grand cas.

Mr. Fox se rendant à Washington pour solliciter des ordres me prie de le recommander à quelqu'un de la Legation. Etant content de lui, je lui donne cette lettre pour vous, dans le cas où vous ayez besoin de ses services, Neuilly le recommander à les messieurs de la Legation.

Je vous rendour elle, cher ami, l'assurance de ma bien bonne amitie.

M't tout affec.
JS. BORER.

J'ai été à même d'apprécier l'élégance des vêtements faits par Mr. Geo. P. Fox et le recommande à M. M. Aluecar, Jom de Bertodanos Ariaga.

WASHINGTON, 1 *Mai*, 1862.

L. DEJARDIN.

431 14th Street.

WASHINGTON, *May* 22, 1866.

Dear Sir,—You have not sent your bill. I hope it is not growing. Please send it.

Can you make me three nice suits of VERY LIGHT AND COMFORTABLE summer clothing, say one black, one white, and one some mixed, but light color?

If some other color than pure black or white will be a better taste, please advise me, also if the coat, half way between sack and frock, should be of different color for part suit; I shall rely on your taste to have everything just right.

Make one suit immediately that I may try fit and style before the others are made.

Please answer immediately,

Yours truly,

S. P. CHASE.

G. P. FOX,
 Merchant Tailor.

WASHINGTON, *May* 7, 1866.

My Dear Sir,—I return you samples here and pinned together which seem to me best, but I have so poor an opinion of my judgment in such matters that I shall be glad to have you exercise your own without regard much to mine.

Instead of one of the three, say the darkest, would it not be better to have a pure black suit? What goods do you use for black?

What I insist on chiefly is *lightness and comfort* in warm weather. The question of having coat, pants, and vest of the same, or different colors, I leave to you.

First, Please make the white suit, or white except coat as you think best, and if possible let me have it this week. If you come to Washington perhaps you will bring it, and then we can decide as to the vest.

It is probable that I shall leave town next week early, perhaps Monday.

Yours truly,
S. P. CHASE.

Mr. G. P. Fox.

Providence, R. I. *Sept.* 1, 1866.

Dear Sir,—Your bill of $557, also $212, reached me here yesterday. Inclosed is check for balance for $345. Please send bill receipted to Washington, where I expect to be after a few days.

Yours respectfully,
S. P. CHASE.

Mr. G. P. Fox.
    Merchant Tailor.

Washington, *Dec.* 4, 1866.

Dear Sir,—The clothes meet general approbation. The shirts, though not expected, did not yet arrive.

Yours respectfully,
S. P. CHASE.

Mr. G. P. Fox.

NAVY DEPARTMENT,
WASHINGTON, *March* 31, 1870.

Sir,—Agreeably to your request, which was referred to this Department by the Hon. James Brooks, I transmit herewith a copy of the Naval Uniform Regulations. A Register will be sent to you as soon as published.

For the other books named in your request, your letter has been referred to the War Department, who will doubtless forward publications which you desired.

Very respectfully,

HOLMES E. OFFEY,
Chief Clerk.

GEORGE P. FOX, Esq.
No. 47 Amity Street, New York.

ADJUTANT GENERAL'S OFFICE,
WASHINGTON, *April* 6, 1870.

HON. JAMES BROOKS, M. C.,
Washington, D. C.

Sir,—I have to return herewith communication from Geo. P. Fox, Esq. No. 47 Amity Street, New York City, together with a copy of the latest edition of the Regular Army Register, and to inform you that there are no copies of the Revised Army Regulations on hand for distribution, the last edition having been exhausted.

I am very respectfully,

Your obedient servant,

E. D. TOWNSEND,
Adjutant General.

DEPARTMENT OF STATE,
WASHINGTON, *April*, 19, 1870.

Sir,—The Secretary of State desires me to acknowledge the receipt of your two letters, bearing date the 22d ultimo, and 16th inst. respectively, and to say in reply that it is not the province of this Department to determine questions of law, such as that propounded in your letter. The information you seek can probably be obtained by application to a competent lawyer.

The accompaniment of your letter of the 22d ultimo is herewith returned.

I am, Sir,

Your obedient servant

R. S. CHEN,
Chief Clerk.

GEORGE P. FOX, Esq..
    47 Amity Street, New York.

ATTORNEY-GENERAL'S OFFICE.
WASHINGTON, *April* 25, 1870.

Sir,—I have received your letter of the 22d inst.

The law does not permit me to give you an official opinion upon the question you ask.

Very respectfully,

E. R. HOAR,
Attorney-General.

GEORGE P. FOX, Esq.,
    No. 47 Amity Street, New York.

EXECUTIVE MANSION,
WASHINGTON, D. C, *May*, 16, 1870.

Sir,—Your letter was referred to the Secretary of State with whom you should communicate in regard to your emblem flag as a trade mark.

I am Sir,

Your obedient servant,

HORACE PORTER.

Secretary.

GEORGE P. FOX, Esq.,
  47 Amity Street, New York.

DEPARTMENT OF STATE,
WASHINGTON, *Sept.* 9, 1871.

GEO. P. FOX, Esq.,
  47 Amity Street, New York.

Sir,—In reply to your letter of the 5th instant, I have to state that, by a resolution of Congress of the 27th of March, 1867, all persons in the diplomatic service of the United States are prohibited from wearing any uniform or official costume.

I am, Sir,

Your obedient servant,

W. HUNTER.

Acting Secretary.

CORRESPONDENCE FROM THE HON. SUN SET COX,

MEMBER OF CONGRESS FROM THE CITY OF NEW YORK.

My Dear Sir,—I am just at home from California.

I have yours of 28th June and have (unless too late) written for the information you desire.

With regards,

S. S. COX.

TO MR. GEO. P. FOX.

If it is proper for the Dept. to give the information, you will get it direct. If you do not get it, it is because the Dept. wont give it for—— State reasons.

NEW YORK, 13 E. 12TH STREET,
 Sept. 17, 1871.

        DEPARTMENT OF STATE,
       WASHINGTON, 22d *Sept.*, 1871.

MY DEAR MR. COX:—

We should be very glad to provide your friend Mr. Fox with a description of the uniform of the diplomatic and consular servants of the Republic; and so far as we are able it is given in the inclosed; but the laws you helped to make, as you perceive, allow only those diplomatic and consular officers who have served in the armies of the United States to wear any uniform. Those who have so served may, if they desire, wear any uniform proper for their military rank or brevet rank.

DIPLOMATIC SERVICE.

INSTRUCTIONS, ACTS OF CONGRESS, &c., TO JULY 28TH, 1866.

§ XXII. Ministers and officers of the several grades in the diplomatic service of the United States are hereby instructed to conform to the requirements of the joint resolution of Congress approved on the 27th of March, 1867, prohibiting them from wearing any uniform or official costume not previously authorized by Congress.

The 34th section of an act approved the 28th of July, 1866, authorizes all officers who have served during the rebellion as volunteers in the armies of the United States to bear the official title, and, upon occasions of ceremony, to wear the uniform of the highest grade they have held by brevet or other commissions in the volunteer service. This section constitutes the exception made in the prohibitory resolution above referred to, and is in full force and effect in its application to persons in the diplomatic or any other branch of the civil service of the United States who may have served in our armies in the manner therein described.

The text of the joint resolution and section before named is as follows:

["PUBLIC RESOLUTION—NO. 15.]

"A RESOLUTION concerning the uniform of persons in the diplomatic service of the United States.

"*Resolved by the Senate and House of Representatives of the United States of America in Congress assembled,* That all persons in the diplomatic service of the United States are prohibited from wearing any uniform or official costume not previously authorized by Congress.

"Approved March 27, 1867."

"SEC. 34. *And be it further enacted,* That all officers who have served during the rebellion as volunteers in the armies of the United States, and who have been, or may hereafter be, honorably mustered out of the volunteer service, shall be entitled to bear the official title, and, upon occasions of ceremony, to wear the uniform of the highest grade they have held by brevet or other commissions in the volunteer service. In case of officers of the regular army, the volunteer rank shall be entered upon the official army register: *Provided,* That these privileges shall not entitle any officer to command, pay, or emoluments."

There was in former years a uniform designed to meet the usages of European courts. At that time, on the recommendation of the mission to Ghent, a description of which is as follows:

MEMORANDUM OF THE DRESS OF AN AMERICAN MINISTER AS FIXED BY THE MISSION TO GHENT.

A blue coat, lined with white silk; straight standing cape, embroidered with gold, single breasted, straight or round button-holes, slightly embroidered. Buttons, plain, or, if they can be had, with the artillerists' eagle stamped upon them—*i. e.*, an eagle flying, with a wreath in its mouth, grasping lightning in one of its talons. Cuffs embroidered in the manner of the cape; white cassimere breeches; gold knee-buckles; white silk stockings; and gold or gilt shoe buckles. A three-cornered chapeau-bras, not so large as those used by the French, nor so small as those of the English. A black cockade, to which lately an eagle has been attached. Sword, &c., corresponding.

The Secretaries have the same costume, with the exception that their coats have less embroidery than that of the Minister.

It is usual, at all European courts, on what are called *gala days*, such as birthdays of the Sovereign, marriages of Princes of his family, and other extraordinary occasions, for the foreign Ministers, as well as other persons of distinction, connected with the court, to appear in uniforms more splendid with embroidery, than upon occasions of ordinary levees, drawing-rooms, and diplomatic circles. A decent respect for the usages of the courts, and a suitable compliance with forms there established, make it proper that the *Minister* of the United States should adopt this custom, and wear, on those occasions, a coat, similar to that above described, but embroidered round the skirts, and down the breasts, as well as at the cuffs and cape—all the other parts of the dress remaining the same. The coats to be distinguished as the *great* and the small uniform. There should be a white ostrich feather, or *plumet*, in the Minister's hat, not standing erect, but sewed round the brim.

All the persons attached to the legation, wear the same uniform as the Secretary, and need to have only one.

DEPARTMENT OF STATE, *Nov. 6th*, 1817.

Governor Marcy, however, in 1853, (June 1st), issued a circular, doing away with such uniforms in a great degree.

(CIRCULAR.)

DEPARTMENT OF STATE,
WASHINGTON, *June* 1, 1853.

In addition to the "Personal Instructions to the Diplomatic Agents of the United States in Foreign Countries," the following are hereafter to be observed:

In performing the ceremonies observed upon the occasion of his reception, the Representative of the United States will conform, as far as is consistent with a just sense of his devotion to republican institutions, to the customs of the country wherein he is to reside, and with the rules prescribed for Representatives of his rank; but the Department would encourage, as far as practicable, without impairing his usefulness to his country, his appearance at court in the simple dress of an American citizen. Should there be cases where this cannot be done, owing to the character of the Foreign Government, without detriment to the public interest, the nearest approach to it compatible with the due performance of his duties is earnestly recommended. The simplicity of our usages and the tone of feeling among our people is much more in accordance with the example of our first and most distinguished Representative at a royal court than the practice which has since prevailed. It is to be regretted that there was ever any departure in this respect from the example of Dr. Franklin. History has recorded and commended this example, so congenial to the spirit of our political institutions. The Department is desirous of removing all obstacles to a return to the simple and unostentatious course which was deemed so proper and was so much approved in the earliest days of the Republic. It is our purpose to cultivate the most amicable relations with all countries, and this we believe can be effectually done without requiring our diplomatic agents abroad to depart in this respect from what is suited to the general sentiments of our fellow-citizens at home. All instructions in regard to what is called diplomatic uniform or court-dress being withdrawn, each of our

Representatives in other countries will be left to regulate this matter according to his own sense of propriety, and with a due respect to the views of his Government as herein expressed.

It is desirable that the Minister or Chargé d'Affairs should establish the Legation in as central a position as may be convenient of the Metropolis near the Government to which he is sent. It will be his duty to see that it is kept open every day, except Sundays and fête days, from 9 o'clock in the forenoon until 3 o'clock in the afternoon. The Secretary attached to it, if there be one, must perform, in person, all the services which properly devolve upon him, except in cases of sickness or leave of absence. In such cases, it is enjoined upon the Minister to appoint an American citizen to represent him, if it can be done. There is an obvious impropriety in devolving upon a foreigner the duties which belong to the Secretary. It is necessary to be thus specific in these instructions; for it has frequently occurred, of latter years, that Secretaries of Legation have, as this Department is informed, employed clerks whose allegiance was foreign to copy dispatches and do other official duties which pertained to themselves. This practice, which it is feared is upon the increase, is so obviously wrong, that the President is resolved to cause it to be discontinued. The correspondence between the Government and the Legations of the United States must be guarded with the utmost secrecy even as relates to our own citizens. To submit it to the examination of a foreigner will be regarded as an indiscretion in the offender demanding immediate deprivation of office. The first duty of a subject is considered to be fidelity to his Sovereign. Foreign clerks may justly be regarded as unsafe depositaries of the secrets of our diplomacy in the Legation where they are employed. The possibility that a revelation of our secret State papers may occur in this manner is sufficient to excite fears on the subject and require the strict observance of the above instructions.

Ministers of the United States and Chargés d'Affairs are requested to authenticate, by their own signatures, with the seal of the Legation, the passports of American citizens, and not permit Secretaries to perform this duty when they themselves are at their posts.

W. L. MARCY.

Then, in 1867, Congress brought its wisdom to bear on the question, and prohibited all but military uniforms, as above stated, as you will see by reference to inclosure.

I leave it with you to settle the question with your friend Fox, who, I am afraid, will be disappointed as to the extent of the field for supplying diplomatic costume.

Always truly yours,

R. S. CHEW.

THE HONORABLE S. S. COX,
New York City.

CRITICISMS OF AMERICAN AND ENGLISH JOURNALS.

NOTICES OF THE PRESS ON THE PRESENT AND FORMER EDITIONS OF THIS WORK, &c., &c—FASHION AND POLITICS IN WASHINGTON—FROM AN OCCASIONAL CORRESPONDENT, "NEW YORK EXPRESS."

WASHINGTON, *Jan.*—, 1861.

Another week of excitement has passed, and the country is still comparatively safe. How long this sense of security will remain, depends upon an immediate decisive convention and a delegation to Washington of the sovereign people of all the States—East, West, North and South, and somewhat upon our representatives (query *mis*-representatives) in Congress, the politicians out of it, and the developments of time and future events. Notwithstanding the distractions which have come upon us, the people in this metropolis seem prone to enjoy the usual festivities of this season of the year, just as if the secession movement had never been talked of, and as if there was no embarrassment at all to our national prosperity. The President's series of levees was inaugurated on the 15th, in a style of brilliancy equal to any which have preceded it, and a large company entered into the gaieties of the occasion with a zest equal to the best days of that democratic institution, a social reunion at the Presidential mansion. The President seemed in excellent spirits, a fact which appeared to give satisfactory evidence to his visitors that he, at least, does not yet despair of bringing the ship of State safely into the haven of peace, and all in good season. The Cabinet was represented by Secretary Black and lady, Attorney-General Stanton, and Secretary Holt, and Hon. Horatio King. The Diplomatic corps were out in full force, the representatives from the Courts of St. James, Russia, Austria, Prussia, Belgium, Sweden, Brazil, Spain, and other ministers being present.

Among the distinguished civilians present, Mr. Geo. P. Fox, the celebrated tailor of New York, and leader of Fashion, attracted attention by his gentlemanly bearing and the unequalled magnificence of his attire. Mr. Fox proved himself upon this occasion, as he has always done on every other, pre-eminently the Leader of Fashion; and a description of his *tout ensemble* may prove interesting even in these days of war's alarms and disagreeable sensations. In this connection I may mention that Mr. Fox had already created a sensation in fashionable circles before his appearance at the levee, by the princely order of his street costume, appearing alternately in some instances in half a dozen different fashionable suits of clothes in the course of a day. There has appeared to be no end to the variety, extent and richness of his wardrobe, and it became really a matter of speculation whether he could produce anything new for the gathering at the Presidential levee. Some one, a wag undoubtedly, intimated that Mr. Fox would be obliged to appear in a *shroud* at the levee, for it seemed as if he had exhausted all the novelty in the way of mundane habiliments, and would be obliged to have recourse to the *outré* garb alluded to, to produce a further sensation. Strange to relate, the Leader of Fashion *did* attend the levee in the material of a *shroud*, being clothed in a blue cloth dress-coat, manufactured from the identical piece from which Mr. Fox formed the citizen dress, while living, and the grave-clothes, after death, of the patriotic Webster; this garment was *à la mode*, with blue velvet skirt linings, and ornamented with gold buttons. The rest of the costume was in keeping, and was as follows: brimstone buff satin dress-vest; black dress cassimere pantaloons; frill shirt, with ruffle sleeves; white neck-tie, with valencia ends; white kid gloves, black silk stockings, dress pumps. In addition to this beautiful attire, Mr. Fox wore to the White House a military scarlet K'haban envelope, lined with scarlet silk and velvet, richly trimmed with gold and ermine fur collar and cuffs; United States officer's chapeau, with a plume of red, white, blue and buff feathers; United States regulation sword and belt. Such was the Leader of Fashion's attractive and extremely tasteful outfit for the gay assemblage at the White House, and is it at all singular that the wearer should have been the observed of all observers, even in that throng where the great effort has always been to see who shall appear to the best advantage? While on this subject of dress, I may mention that Mr. Fox has appeared here, dressed in the distinctive costumes of the Diplomatic corps, and in that of the Army and Navy officers, as well as in the ordinary garb of the gentleman of taste of the present day.

This advent of Mr. Fox, who was driven to the White House in a magnificent carriage drawn by splendid gray horses, to and from Willard's Hotel, created at once a sensation. Politics gave way to fashion, and the leaders of party seemed instinctively to bow in admiration of the genius of the man who could thus create a sentiment which surmounted even the asperities of political antagonism. Mr. Fox was presented to the President by Deputy Marshal Phillips, and after an exchange of those courtesies usual on the occasion, was introduced to Miss Lane by Commissioner Blake. To Miss L. Mr. Fox presented a beautiful bouquet, somewhat to her embarrassment, it appeared, for she already held in her hand another bunch of culled sweets. But with that delicacy and tact which is her leading characteristic, she blushed, and passed to a lady friend the bouquet which she had, and retained the pleasing gift of fashion's leader.*

To the bouquet was attached a card containing the following impromptu effusion:

> "For flowers like these three maids divine contended;
> For flowers like these Eve's glorious hours were ended.
> Had you been there, the contest ne'er had pended;
> Had you been there, the angel had relented."

On the obverse appeared the following patriotic sentiment:

"MORE MEANT THAN MEETS THE EAR.

" Let fashion and fashioners frown down, and immediately try to avert all and every malign influence that at the present time endangers the peace, progress and prosperity of the United States."

Beneath this sentiment was drawn a symbol of our Union, a perfect circle, with the four important chronological events in our nation's history, viz: 1492, the discovery of the country; 1732, the birth of Washington; 1776, the Declaration of Independence, and the present year, 1861; inside the Union circle appeared the cardinal points of the compass. The gift was very appropriate, and afforded the fair recipient much pleasure. The Diplomatic corps, the gentlemen acquaintances and lady friends of Miss Lane, found much food for conversation and enjoyment in this incident of the levee. The former were struck with the masterly stroke of diplomacy, which secured so much attention, and were little inclined to be envious, but they bore their defeat becomingly, and universally admitted that the act was perfectly in keeping, and worthy of the man. The ladies appeared to covet the gift, and seemed divided in their admiration of the compliment to Miss L., and the delicacy of the conception which dictated it.

* It was the patriotic bouquet of the season. In the centre were apple-blossoms, an emblem of the garden of Eden; while around the centre appeared the olive, the carmel, the almond, the heliotrope, all significant of the glory of the country, and a trust in the ultimate obliteration of all our national troubles, through a peaceful victory.

In the course of his sojourn in this city, Mr. Fox has been in familiar conversation with a large number of our most eminent statesmen and citizens, who were quite as anxious to gather views upon the existing complications in our government, as upon the various topics connected with the world of fashion. Coming so freshly from the people, Mr. F. has been enabled to impart such correct information in regard to the public sentiment in New York, as has been, no doubt, acceptable and valuable to many of our national legislators, officials and others. Among these I may mention the President and Vice-President, Senators Crittenden, Douglas, Gwin, Sumner, King and Latham; the Secretary of the Navy, Hon. Horatio King, Hon. John A. Dix, General Cass, Hon. J. B. Adrain, Hon. John L. N. Stratton, Hon. John Cochrane, Hon. Dwight Loomis, Hon. John Woodruff, Hon. Reverdy Johnson, Col. Kane, Commissioner from South Carolina; General Harney, U. S. A.; Col. Cooper. Adj. Gen. U. S. A.; Col. Keys, Military Secretary to Lt. Gen. Scott; Hon. John A. Gurley, Hon. John Sherman, Professor S. F. Baird, and many others. I allude to these merely to show how actively the time of Mr. Fox has been employed, and that he has had opportunity to turn attention to the affairs of our suffering country, as well as to the duties of his peculiar and honorable profession.

On Saturday morning Mr. Fox paid another visit to the White House, and had a more unconstrained interview with the President and Miss Lane. The former expressed his gratification at the call, while the latter uttered her unrestrained pleasure at the compliment at the levee. Mr. F. made a tour of the White House, the conservatory, &c., in company with other distinguished citizens, and departed after a most pleasant interchange of sentiment. On this occasion Mr. F. was dressed in the usual costume of a gentleman making a morning call—morning promenade coat, fancy cassimere vest, and pantaloons seemingly coarse, yet of the finest material. A little episode occurred at this visit, which is worth relating. As Mr. Fox entered the White House, Mr. A. T. Stewart, of

New York, "the Emperor of the rag trade," as he is sometimes called, was leaving. Mutual recognition and exchange of courtesies took place between the leader and one of his chief aids, and the former passed in as the other passed out. On Sunday, Mr. Fox dined at Willard's, and feasted like an old Roman, but with commendable moderation.

I have devoted this much of my letter to the famous leader of fashion, because he is, just now, the sensation here, and has completely divided attention with the national crisis. Mr. Fox is no ordinary individual. He is a man of fine literary ability, and has given to the world an essay on Modern Dress and Fashion of transcendent merit. He may be termed an enthusiast in his profession, somewhat transcendental in the beauty and originality of his ideas, yet strong and vigorous in his conceptions and their execution. In view of Mr. Fox's accomplishments, one may readily believe that, if Cotton is *King*, Fashion is Supreme; and thus closes my essay on Fashion and Politics in the Federal Metropolis.

E. PLURIBUS UNUM.

[From the London Saturday Review.]

A TRANSCENDENTAL TAILOR.

We have long been aware of the perfection to which the Americans have brought advertising. Englishmen may admire their own Moses so long as they remain in Europe, but they must cross the Atlantic if they would behold the highest triumphs of the art of puffing. "The President of Fashion," Mr. George P. Fox, of New York, does this sort of thing in a style which ought to teach Moses & Sons humility. The "Philosophy of Modern Dress" is not indeed a poem, nor does it appear that Mr. Fox's extensive and admirably-organized establishment contains a poet. But perhaps elegant prose is more likely to command general attention. And, besides, Mr. Fox treats his subject in a more enlightened spirit than the firm of Moses. According to them, dress is everything; but Mr. Fox more wisely says that dress with education makes the gentleman. "The air of good Society cannot be given except by education, aided by the artistic hand of a genuine tailor." Thoughtful men will be attracted to an "institution," as Mr. Fox calls it, which puts forward its claims thus moderately, while they will see through the fallacy of the bolder statement that a dress suit from Moses & Sons at £5 5s. will at once turn the purchaser into a gentleman. With education, and "such an outfit as emanates from the popular emporium" of Mr. Fox, you are promised "a delightful sense of social security," and you feel that such a promise may be relied on. You are, perhaps, a little astounded to hear of an "outfit emanating" from an emporium; but if you are, that is a proof that your education has been neglected, and therefore, if your social success should be incomplete, you will know that the fault is in yourself, and not in the "artistic hand" which made your clothes. And, even if you cannot at once scale the highest pinnacle of fashion, there is still much to be gained by putting yourself under Mr. Fox's care.

"No civilized man is apt to commit a crime in a good suit of clothes." Here is a security against roguery offered in an unexpected quarter. It has often been asked—What is to be done to check the course of enormous commercial frauds? How can a board of directors trust its secretary or manager, whom it is powerless to control? The answer is—By requiring him to be fashionably dressed. We sometimes hear a demand for a Government inspection of joint-stock banks. Let us rather employ the Surveyor of the Board of Trade to inspect the garments of the cashiers. "Arrayed in a fine and elegant costume, with the consummate polish of appearance, which it is equally the duty and the pride of the conscientious artist to impart, a man feels his responsibilities as a citizen, is inspired with the love of order, becomes refined and elevated in his tastes, is filled with respect for law, decorum, and propriety, and finds in his own character a guarantee against temptation." Surely this is as convincing as it is eloquent. Do we need Mr. Fox's further assurance that no customer of his has ever been convicted of a crime? He gently complains in another place that men sometimes speak inconsiderately of tailors. We are sure that men of sense will henceforth speak of them with profound respect, and will promote them to the honor and authority which is their due. For let us only consider what a first-rate tailor might have done for us in the Russian war. Instead of numerous officers ineffectually inspecting gun-boats, we should have had a single officer examining the make and fit of the contractors' clothes. If the Gun-boat Committee had read Mr. Fox's pamphlet, they would have closed their Report with a piece of practical advice—that all builders and workmen engaged on contract-built ships should be arrayed in fine and elegant costumes, so that they might find in their own characters, as influenced by the coats upon their backs, a sufficient safeguard against the temptation to defraud an ignorant and careless Board of Admiralty.

Such are some of the arguments in support of Mr. Fox's claims to the confidence of the fashionable world. Let us now see how those arguments are strengthened by authority. The letters which Mr. Fox has received from eminent men about the make and material of their clothes are printed as an appendix to his pamphlet. In the van of this army of exquisites marches the celebrated Daniel Webster, who, "as he was the most able of Constitutionalists, was also one of the best-dressed of gentlemen." He left special directions for his burial in clothes which Mr. Fox made for him. Thus—

<blockquote>Even from the tomb the voice of nature cries—</blockquote>

saying. "Buy your clothes of Mr. Fox." A New York paper told the world that "Those who bent over his coffin recognized that mighty form, robed in the same vest and the same blue dress-coat, with the velvet collar and gold-wove cloth buttons," &c.; and we learn from an affidavit of Mr. Fox, duly sworn, and having a piece of blue cloth annexed, that the pantaloons of black cassimere emanated from the same emporium. There is also a note of Mr. Webster desiring to have his "K'haban" on a particular morning; and another, stating that it is "the most comfortable and easy-fitting summer garment he had ever worn." Mr. Webster's secretary assures Mr. Fox that the great Statesman actually dictated these words; and the same personage also vouches for the fact that "he was interred in his best blue coat," being the identical one which the newspaper above quoted calls "this same chaste, but nobly made, blue dress-coat." We are thankful to the secretary for this statement from an impartial witness, because, on a point of such importance, we could scarcely feel satisfied either with the unsupported affidavit of Mr. Fox, or with a newspaper paragraph the style of which suggests a suspicion that it may have emanated from the emporium in Broadway. On the whole of the evidence, we do not feel any doubt that Mr. Webster was really buried "in the said suit of clothes as above set forth."

With a noble generosity, Mr. Fox sends presents of cloth to distinguished citizens, and then offers to make it up into garments gratis. We understand that Mr. Fox finds his reward in the proud consciousness that he has helped to make a new President and his Ministers look like gentlemen. Mr. Filmore would have been happy to avail himself of one of these kind offers, "but the truth is, I have found it more difficult to procure a perfectly fitting pair of pantaloons than any other garment," and, therefore, he cannot venture to send a pattern. We can fancy how Mr. Fox hereupon gently patronized the President, and taught him not to be ashamed of his own legs in his own drawing-room. Ambition too often ends in disappointment, but ex-President Filmore carried with him into his retirement that peace of mind and ease of movement which were derived from the consciousness of being well-dressed. Another President, General Pierce, was treated with even more attention. Mr. Fox measured and fitted him by the eye, and his secretary wrote that "the garments were all admirably adapted to the figure," and that the President appreciated the generosity of the gift. We may say that we appreciate it also, although not exactly at the figure which Mr. Fox would like. We cannot help thinking of how Sam Slick sold clocks, when we read, under date of the next year, that "the President's coachman and footman are in need of box-coats for summer." They are to have pocket-flaps "to give the coat a distinctive character as a box-coat," and Mr. Fox may also send pants of the same material. We learn from other letters, that the Hon. S. A. Douglas paid his bill; that Commodore Perry preferred English lace on his coat and pantaloons; that the Sergeant-at-Arms of the Senate found that his clothes "fitted with all the ease of an old suit, while they exhibited all the polish of a new," and that a lady had said that the same clothes were "neatly beautiful;" that it would have been convenient to the Hon. Edward Everett, to receive at a particular time, the garments he had ordered of Mr. Fox; that Sir H. L. Bulwer would have liked to suggest a few small alterations in his trousers; that Sir John F. Crampton paid his bill, and also that of Mr. Bulwer Lytton, "the son of Sir Edward Bulwer Lytton, Bart.," and desired to have receipts; and that Mdlle. Jenny Lind wanted a gentleman's morning-wrapper. It also appears that Mr. Fox presented "a superb suit of black cloth clothes to Father Mathew, and a very handsome and costly gift" to T. F. Meagher, who presented him in return with a copy of his speeches; but whether or not the paper on which they were printed was large enough to cut up into patterns we are left in doubt.

A Washington paper states that at a levee, "Mr. Fox's style made quite an impression on our fashionables." In another sense of the word, Mr. Fox's style has made quite an impression on ourselves. There was an interchange of salutations on the occasion between the President of the States, Mr. Filmore, and the President of Fashion, Mr. Fox, who were the two lions of the day. We should think that Mr. Filmore, conscious of ill-fitting pants, must have been a very tame lion under the all-judging eye of Mr. Fox. But it rather appears that this levee was held after the President's wardrobe had been remodelled; and Mr. Fox probably came there to gaze with quiet pleasure at his own good work, and to behold, in Mr. Filmore's blue coat, fancy vest, and black cassimere pantaloons, one more triumph of that great career in which "he has adorned the Doric simplicity of American principles by the inimitable grace and elegance of an appropriate Democratic costume." We own with humiliation that Mr. Moses has never proposed to himself an aim so noble, nor stated it in language so majestic; nor has his mind grasped that principle on which Mr. Fox insists strongly—that "a ready-made garment is, according to the laws of good taste, an impossibility." We are inclined to think that "a free ticket to the best places of society" emanates only from the emporium in Broadway.

NEW PUBLICATIONS.

THE COSMOPOLITAN INVENTOR.—THE PHILOSOPHY OF MODERN DRESS AND FASHION, BY MR. GEO. P. FOX, OF THIS CITY.

We have had an opportunity of perusing the advance sheets of his work, 3d Edition, Series A.D. 1850, 1860, 1871. We give it as our opinion that it is a work that will command an immense circulation both here and in Europe, on account of its great merit, more especially as the author, who owns and controls the publication, will permit the same to be offered to the public at prices within the reach of all. We understand that Mr. Fox intends to place the book on sale with the most prominent booksellers of this city and throughout the country. Reprints of the edition will appear also in London, Paris and other European cities. We perceive that the principal N. Y. journals are taking an unusual interest in publishing extracts from the edition. The author handles the subject like an adept in polite and elegant literature. It is asserted that he gra uated from the humble rank of a printer's devil, as ink-boy, to the more progressive positions of letter-press and copperplate printer, engraver and paper maker, as a proprietor. In this he was aided, in the year 1843, by his own inventions on certain civilizing pieces of machinery, and in improvements of a marked character, such as the steam-engine valves. Also, on the atmospheric cylinder, known as the American paper machine, including improvements on Foudrinier's Longitudinal and Cross-cut paper-cutting machine, &c. Singular to relate, that the comparatively new 6th order of architecture, technically known as the "Cosmopolitan," originated with Mr. Fox, who showed to the world, for the first time, in the year 1841, newly-invented improvements, with brief specifications which were entered by him in pamphlet form at Stationer's Hall, London. These were afterwards known as the Union base principle, or Cosmopolitan order of Architecture, and more especially as applied to the construction of the front elevation of mercantile edifices. This improved form of structure came into vogue in this city about the year 1852. This style of construction was first shown* at 43 Dean's Gate North, Manchester, England, and then in an imperfect manner, and afterwards it was pirated from his plans and working drawings, as seen in the large five-story building owned by the late Mr. Strong, northwest corner of Broadway and Waverley Place, some years since occupied by Mr. Wm. Jackson as a dry-goods store, and at present known as Mr. Jackson's mourning establishment. One of the prominent mercantile structures showing this order of architecture in a more extended form is the iron front and oblong building owned and occupied by the firm of Messrs. A. T. Stewart & Co., covering the whole block (say two acres), on 9th and 10th streets, Broadway and 4th avenue. The common observer will notice the uniformity of elevation of the cosmopolitan style of architecture. The so-called "Emperor of the Dry-Goods trade," Mr. A. T. Stewart, is, therefore, largely indebted to the so-called "Leader of Fashion" and "'Transcendental Tailor," to use the language of the London *Saturday Review.* Mr. Fox claims to have originated the idea of showing how to construct grand, imposing and magnificent mercantile edifices, the finest of their kind on the continent of America or in Europe or elsewhere.

* Geo. Fox & Co., Merchant Tailor and Outfitting Establishment, 1835—1846. Geo. P. Fox, sole proprietor; no partner other than his late lamented wife Mary.

GEORGE P. FOX STILL LIVES.

[From the N. Y. Express, July 7, 1871.]

Our old Merchant Tailor, long the leader of fashions in New York, appeared July 4th, 1871, in his celebrated U. S. costumes of Commanding Lieutenant, S. N. U., then as Grand Admiral, then as a Commander-in-chief S. A. U., and finally as the Emperor of Fashion, in which he wore his grand scarlet coat, a very costly, rich and beautiful garment, designed and made by him in 1852. He rode in a four-horse open barouche, decorated with a rare and unique international banner, on which were represented the flags of all nations. A streamer from the same staff bore the words: "*Faire sans dire.*" "*Ventus secundus.*" On the front seat was a stuffed fox, appearing as upon a full run, with a rooster's head in his mouth, and the body on his back. The American Eagle surmounted the flag-staff. The whole presented a very marked and attractive appearance.

Easter Monday he was invited to appear in the German procession, at the head of the column, and, saluting the Grand Army and Cavalry escort, consisting of over sixty-two thousand men, was honored, in return, by the representatives of William, Bismarck, Moltke, Our Fritz and the other Princes, and as "the Leader of Fashion." St. Patrick's Day, March 17, also Mr. Fox's birthday), Mr. Fox turned out with eleven horses, an open barouche, with four horses, taking the lead. A private two horse-carriage, with blinds-drawn, followed. Then came the yacht "City of Ragusa," on a truck drawn by four horses, Grand Admiral Fox commanding and giving his orders to captain and crew as if upon old ocean. Then came the baggage-wagon, with all of the costume dresses of the leader of fashion, the whole being an escort to the Hibernians and all the Sons of St. Patrick, consisting of an army of over forty thousand men. Mr. Fox designs in a short time, as early as September, 1871, to introduce in several numbers, his work on "The Philosophy of Modern Dress and Fashion," upon which he has expended a great deal of time and money. The advance sheets of this work have already been favorably noticed by the press.

569 Broadway, Cor. Prince St., New York,
October 18*th,* 1871.

George P. Fox, Esq :—

Dear Sir,—Recollecting with pleasure your various well-known essays on Dress and Fashion, A. D. 1850 and 1860, and seeing, by the journal notices, your intention of revising and enlarging your work up to 1872, I desire to submit the following:

I thank you for the kind interest you have taken in my behalf to obtain a contract for me to supply your wealthy friend with a bill of goods in my line, known as under-dress and men's furnishing, &c.; and as I am informed that your friend proposes to take a voyage round the world, I am prepared to exhibit samples and supplies of all description of imported fabrics, &c., deemed suitable and requisite for that gentleman's wardrobe.

You will perceive that the under-mentioned schedule contains descriptions of every supposed necessary article requisite for all climates, and for the adornment of his person (a la mode) when calling to pay his respects to the heads of the various Governments during his sojourn, etc.

Before submitting the schedule to your friend, I should feel myself honored if you will do me the favor to call at my establishment as above, and give it your personal inspection, also any additional information appertaining to contemplated changes of fashion, &c., remarking that I have left space on the margin for your friend to mark the quantity of each or any article he may desire.

I am yours, very respectfully,

C. W. FRENCH.

MEMORANDUM SCHEDULE OF GENTLEMEN'S FURNISHING GOODS, &c.

White Cambric Ties Plain.
White Cambric Ties Embroidered.
White Corded Silk Ties.
Black Corded Silk Ties.
Fancy Colored Windsor Scarfs.
Black Silk Scarfs, Pointed and Fringed Ends.
Morning Breakfast Jackets.
French Cardigan Jackets.
Morning Robe de Chambres.
Prince Arthur Colored Shirts.
Embroidered White Linen Shirts.
Plain White Linen Shirts.
White Muslin Fine Shirts.
Linen Night Shirts (Ruffled).
Muslin Night Shirts (Plain).
Excelsior Linen Collars assorted Colors.
Van Buest and other Mode, in Colors.
Reversible Linen Cuffs.
Oxford Linen Cuffs.
Oxford Scarf, Plain and Fancy Colors.
Prince Teck Scarf, Plain and Fancy Colors.
Silk Pocket Handkerchiefs.
White Linen Cambrick Handkerchiefs.
Balbrigan $\frac{1}{2}$ Hose.
The Best Merino $\frac{1}{2}$ Hose, Assorted Shades.

Light Kid Gloves, a la mode.
Dark Kid Gloves,   "
Castor and Buckskin Gloves, a la mode.
6 Thread Double-breasted Merino White Under Shirts.
Gauze Merino Single-breasted White Under Shirts.
Thick 18 Thread Silk Under Shirts.
Thin 3 Thread Silk Under Shirts.
6 Thread Merino Drawers.
Gauze Merino Drawers.
18 Thread Silk Drawers.
3 Thread Silk Drawers.
8 and 12 Ribbed Twilled Silk Umbrella.
Pemento-Mode Walking Sticks.
English Travelling Rugs.
Scotch Travelling Shawls.
Sets Plain Gold and Agate Studs.
Sets Stone Cameo Sleeve Buttons.
Plain Gold Neck Studs.
Fancy Coral Scarf Pins.
Besantien Scarf Pins.
Stone Cameo Scarf Pins.
Suspenders according to taste or requirement.
12 Thread Silk ½ Hose.
3 Thread Silk ½ Hose.
Mode Silk Gloves.
Viesma Portmonaies (Russia Leather).
Glove Boxes (Russia Leather).
Handkerchief Boxes (Russia Leather).
Cigar Cases and Match Boxes.
Toilet Dressing Case complete.
Card Cases—a la mode.

PREAMBLE.

HEAD AND FOOT COVERING.

The author expected in the outset to confine himself more particularly to the subject of outer garments, viz., clothing, but submits the following as a list of the latest description of styles of foot and head covering for a gentleman of wealth and refinement who is about taking a voyage " round the world," and who, during his absence from his home, New York, and not wishing to be short of any needed article of attire during his sojourn on board his own steam yacht, provides his *valet de chambre* with the essentials of a polished gentleman's wardrobe.

The following has been furnished us by the firm of Messrs. Hunt & Dusenbury, of Nos. 3, 4 and 5 Astor House, importers and dealers in hats, caps, &c., Broadway, New York.

SCHEDULE No. 2.

Canvas Oil Skin Sou'wester, with Oil Skin Storm Jacket, Overcoat, Over-all Trousers to match; the same in India-rubber Water-proof Fabric.

Cloth Travelling Caps, with Oil Silk Covers in U. S. N., old regulation pattern.

Cloth Boat-race Caps.

Black Silk Pocket Caps.

Corduroy Duck-shooting Caps.

Cotton Velvet Duck-shooting Caps.

Fancy-colored Silk Horse-racing Caps.

Dark and Light-colored Felt Soft Travelling Hats

Ordinary Straw Hats.

Fine Panama Straw Hats.

Dark and Light Shades of Cloth Soft Hats.

Morning and Evening Dress Hats, Felt, Silk and Beaver, suitable for the Seasons, including the Opera Hat, also appropriate Cases, all a la mode.

———

GENTLEMEN'S BOOT-MAKER, 23D STREET, BROADWAY, OPPOSITE MADISON PARK, NEW YORK CITY.

SCHEDULE No. 3.

House Slippers, No. 1.

Gaiter, Our Fritz (just out), No. 7.

Oxford Tie Shoe, No. 10.

Broad Strap Shoe, No. 13.

Balmoral Laced English Shoe, No. 16.

Buckled English Shoe, No. 65.

Webster Tie Shoe, No 29.

Congress Gaiter Shoe, No. 8.

Hunting Gaiter Shoe, No. 20.

Low-buttoned Shoe, No. 12.

Imitation Button Shoe, No. 2.

Scotch Gaiter, No. 15.

Dress Calf Boot, No. 1.

Patent Leather Boots, No. 1½.

Riding Boot, No. 9.

Napoleon Boot, No. 23.

Dress and Dancing Pumps, No. 21.

Sea-going Salt Water Boots, No. 22.

Hunting Boot, No. 20.

As a matter of course, the polite reader will readily understand that the enumerations of articles, contained in schedules, Nos. 1, 2 and 3, are to be looked upon in the character of a catalogue, showing parts of gentlemen's attire, so that in the hurry of further engagements we may refer to the same, when needing any articles, as above stated. It would be preposterous to suppose that a refined gentleman of elegant leisure would have a wardrobe the size of a merchant tailor's shop, &c. "Cut your coat according to your cloth," and, by all means, live within your means. Enough said to the poor and the rich of all the world.

FINIS

INDEX.

INDEX.

	PAGE
AMERICAN familiarity	72
Avoid ridicule upon religious subjects	77
A moderately well-informed lady, etc.	81
A true gentleman should not take	90
A man is a fool to be dishonest	96
A lady has the right at the latest moment to	91
Author and Mr. John Bull	100
An English philosopher is	120
Attitudes of the Venus, beautiful in the	157
Action! Action!	167
Affectation	171
A father's object	173
Aim high	177
African race, and taxes	182

B

	PAGE
BURKE, EDMOND, the great orator	20
Berlin	23
Brummell, Beau	29
Bonaparte, to the disgust of	112
Black, the color of darkness	145
Blind man, to liken his notion of	147
Bacon, the great moralist, is	163
Bulwer, Sir H. L.	215

	PAGE
CLOTHES and Clothing	17
Complexion, Miss Jones	27
Charles I., king of England	31
Cleanliness, order, for the proprieties of life	41
Clergy, special dress for	56
Catholic Church, vestments of, never vary	57
Church, congratulations not to be offered in	64
Cleanliness and good manners	71
Conversational powers are not given to all	76
China. The people were roused to fury	108
Chesterfield, Lord, writing to	159
Cicero's treatise upon old age	162
Correspondence	199
Commissioners of Emigration and Charity, so-called	185
Castle Garden Emigrant Depot	186
Corwin, Hon. Thomas	211
Chase, Chief Justice S. P.	225
Cox, Hon. S. S.	228

D

	PAGE
DRESS-MAKER	22
Dress, sarcasm levelled against	25
D'Orsey, Count, in recent day	30
Dress, American *vs.* European	36
Dress Coat indispensable in the ball-room	51
Dress universally adopted, etc.	54
Dressed well	55
Dishonorable and dishonored	98
Diogenes was not anything the more	119
Douglas, Hon. Stephen A.	203
Desjardin (of the French Legation)	220

E

	PAGE
EARL OF ESSEX	25
Earl of Harrington	29
European sovereigns	53
English constraint	72
Eat with a fork instead of a knife	77
Evil-doers, a short shift and a hoist	101
Eighteenth century	108
Tattooed skin	117
Egyptian linen, texture of	123

F

	PAGE
Far off his coming shines	18
Fox, Charles James, British Commoner	20
Fashion: let it follow the treasures of the U. S.	22
Fenelon, Archbishop	25
Fox, George P. It is no use to con, etc.	27
Fire Department, New York	35
Fenelon's maxim	78
Fashion was not to be so ruled by	109
Fashion, the English and French	114
Fashion, the most ancient with	116
Fashion has been defined	118
Foot covering	121
Fop—vanity	143
Frivolous, the French	161
Fillmore, Millard, Ex-President	204, 205

	PAGE
GOOD exterior may become...................................	26
Golden ball introduced black velvet suits.....................	53
Gentleman, what constitutes a	69
Gentleman should not ask.....................	83
George III., the tyrant......................................	104
Gustavus of Sweden..	111
Graham, Dr., the fashionable, when consulted	115
Gold gamblers	187
Greeley, Hon. Horace.........	212

H

	PAGE
How remarkable well you look to-day	28
Hunter, English, a picture of manliness	50
Hambleton and Argyle, arms of the family	65
Horseback, accompanying a lady	88
He that gathereth by labor, etc.	94
Honest advocate, foundation stone of	97
History repeats itself: "Necessity knows no law"	102
Head covering	121
His six spanking grays	130
Had not learned unblushingly to confide	133
Hazlitt says, "Fashion constantly begins and ends in two things,"	139
How to be considerable	168
Hampden a lesson	175
Hoar, Hon. E. R. (Attorney-General)	227

I

	PAGE
INTRODUCTIONS by the consent of.............................	73
Invited guests first seek the lady of the house	74
If a guest is particularly amusing, etc.........................	76
Imperial Nash's rule absolute................................	134
I have been in town and bring you the last................	142
Infant, the proportions of the form of, are...................	152
I am sure you know that breaking your word is	163
Insults and injuries...	165

J

JEWELS of silver and jewels of gold borrowed by the Israelites from the Egyptians.. 113
James I., the cloak... 129
Jackal resided in the Indian jungle 141
Juno, form and proportions..................................... 150

K

KINGSMAN, Col., witty 28
King Nush, like all popular monarchs 131

L

	PAGE
LET his dulness	78
Laugh and applaud in right place	79
Legislature found it necessary to interfere	112
Lying	105
Learning and politeness	174
Lind, Jenny	215
Lytton, Bulwer ("Owen Meredith")	210

M

	PAGE
MERCHANT	22
Marlborough before the battle of Blenheim	31
Militia, New York State, etc.	35
Marcy, late Mr.	37
Marshals, U. S., wore a badge	59
Mourning worn for relatives, length of time	68
Marks the untaught savage of	107
Moorish women of Barbary	124
Medean dress, a loose, flowing robe	124
Macaroni, or highly dressed beau of	138
Manners, advantage of	168
Moral character	175

	PAGE
NAPOLEON I., restored, etc.	31
Navies of England and France	33
Noailles as chief de la mode	40
Never offer your hand to	74
Never become a lecturer in polite social circles	75
Napoleon I.—England a nation of shopkeepers	100
Neck, and sometimes wrists, also ankles	122
Nash was a shrewd and inveterate censor of	133
No one contemptible	169
Necessary accomplishments	176
Now that I have got a pig and a cow	188

Out-door relief office of Third Avenue...... 186

P

	PAGE
PETERSHAM, LORD	29
Police, New York	35
Park, Central, New York	46
Park, Hyde, England	46
Polite as a Frenchman	71
Pope beautifully expresses	95
Pen more powerful than the sword	101
Persians, ancient, was	124
Pericles from the time of	125
Peruke, of French origin, had	129
Politicians and Fourth-of-July stump orators	181
Political.—New honest party	184
Perry, Commodore, M. C.	209, 210

Q

	PAGE
QUEEN ELIZABETH, the reign of	27
Queen Elizabeth	109
Queen Elizabeth, the reign of	55

R

RICHELIEU	25
Raleigh, Walter, and others	25
Regulation and dress of the U. S. Army and Navy	32
Richard III. easily concealed	40
Romans made their garments chiefly	126
Recherches sur les costumes	129
Reminiscences from 1831 to 1851	138
Railroads and fraudulent stock speculators	187

	PAGE
SCULPTURE	24
Smith is a good fellow when you know him	26
Secretaries of legation and foreign consuls	37
Scott, General, to fit and suit his form	39
Supreme Court, Judges of U. S.	58
Sheriff, New York, wore a sword and cockade	59
Shaftesbury once wrote	70
Shears	101
Supplement Series	105
Sultan Mahmoud ordered	111
Smock-frocks, the Norman cavaliers took from	117
Such is the intimate relation between the body and the mind,	158

T

	PAGE
Taste is, in fact, like good music	19
The tailor and the dress maker	22
The great Christian maxim, "Do unto others"	93
Turks would not allow	110
The bath was the first fashionable resort in the	132
The formalities received a severe blow at the French Revolution,	135
The well-bred man feels	165
Temper	172
Townsend, Hon. E. D. (Adjutant General)	226

U

PAGE

UNIFORM continued through the reign of James, William, and
Ann.. 31
Uniform does not make the soldier 58

V

VIRTUE is often found in the wardrobe...................... 22
Verdingles debate in Parliament............................ 110
Virginia tobacco—Sir Walter Raleigh 118
Vulgar scoffers 167

	PAGE
WASHINGTON, GENERAL, was celebrated	30
Wellington, Duke of, in 1871	33
Wales, Prince of	41
Wine, do not press upon	77
Who delight in false weights and measures	94
When he first undertook the government of Bath	131
Wellington boots	137
White the color of the day	145
Woman	169
Washington, George, and the early revolutionary Fathers	183
When you are sure you are right, go ahead, etc.	188
Webster, Daniel	199, 200, 202
Webster, Hon. Sidney	206, 207
When in Rome do us Rome does	185
Ward's Island, etc.	186

YOUNG AMERICA too often	191

www.ingramcontent.com/pod-product-compliance
Lightning Source LLC
Chambersburg PA
CBHW031931230426
43672CB00010B/1891